ANDREW MURRAY

EXPERIENCING
THE
HOLY SPIRIT

TABLE OF CONTENTS

PREFACE

In olden times believers met God, knew Him, walked with Him, had the clear and full consciousness that they had dealings with the God of heaven, and had, too, through faith, the assurance that they and their lives were well pleasing to Him. When the Son of God came to earth, and revealed the Father, it was that such intercourse with God, and the assurance of His favor, might become clearer, and be the abiding portion of every child of God. When He was exalted to the Throne of Glory, it was that He might send down into our hearts the Holy Spirit, in whom the Father and the Son have their own blessed life in heaven, to maintain in us, in Divine power, the blessed life of fellowship with God. It was to be one of the marks of the New Covenant that each member of it should walk in personal communion with God. ' They shall teach no more every man his neighbour, Know the Lord; for they shall all know me, from the least to the greatest of them, saith the Lord; for I will forgive their iniquity! 'The personal fellowship and knowledge of God in the Holy Spirit was to be the fruit of the pardon of sin. The Spirit of God's own Son, sent into our hearts to do each moment a work as Divine as the work of the Son in redeeming us, to displace our life and replace it by the life of Christ in power, to make the Son of God divinely and consciously present with us always--this was what the Father had promised as the distinctive blessing of the New Testament. The fellowship of God as the Three One was now to be within us; the Spirit revealing the Son in us, and through Him the Father.

That there are but few believers who realize this walk with God, this life in God, such as their Father has prepared for them, no one will deny. Nor will it admit of dispute what the cause of this failure is, It is acknowledged on all hands that the Holy Spirit, through whose Divine Omnipotence this inner revelation of the Son and the Father in the life and the likeness of the believer is to take place is not known or acknowledged in the Church as He should be. In our preaching and in our practice He does not hold that place of prominence which He has in God's plan and in His promises. While our creed on the Holy Spirit is orthodox and scriptural, His presence and power in the life of believers, in the ministry of the word, in the witness of the Church to the world, is not what the word promises or God's plan requires.

There are not a few who are conscious of this great need, and earnestly ask to know God's mind concerning it, and the way of deliverance out of it. Some feel that their own life is not what it should and might be. Many of them can look back to some special season of spiritual revival, when their whole life was apparently lifted to a higher level. The experience of the joy and strength of the Saviour's presence, as they learned that He would keep them trusting, was, for a time, most real and blessed. But it did not last: there was a very gradual decline to a lower stage, with much of vain effort and sad failure. They would fain know where the evil lies. There can be little doubt that the answer must be this: they did not know or honour the Indwelling Spirit as the strength of their life, as the power of their faith, to keep them always looking to Jesus and trusting in Him. They knew not what it was, day by day, to wait in lowly reverence for the Holy Spirit to deliver from the power of the flesh, and to maintain the wonderful presence of the Father and the Son within them.

There are many more, tens of thousands of God's dear children, who as yet know little of any even temporary experiences of a brighter life than one of never-ending stumbling and rising. They have lived outside of revivals and conferences; the teaching they receive is not specially helpful in the matter of entire consecration. Their surroundings are not favourable to the growth of the spiritual life. There is many an hour of earnest longing to live more according to the will of God, but the prospect of its being really possible to walk and please God, worthy of the Lord to all well pleasing has hardly dawned upon them. To the best part of their birthright as God's children, to the most precious gift of the Father's love in Christ, the gift of the Holy Spirit, to dwell in them, and to lead them, they are practically strangers.

I would indeed count it an unspeakable privilege if my God would use me to bring to these His beloved children the question of His Word: 'Know ye not that ye are a temple of God, and that the Spirit of God dwelleth in you?' and then to tell them the blessed news of what that glorious work is which this Spirit, whom they have within them, is able to do in each of them. I would if I might, show them what it is that has hitherto hindered that Spirit from doing His blessed work, and how divinely simple the path is by which each upright soul can enter into the joy of all that He has been given to work within us, even the full revelation of the presence of the Indwelling Jesus. I have humbly, asked my God that He would give, even in my feeble words, the quickening of His Holy Spirit, that through them the Thoughts and the Truth, the Love and the Power of God, may enter and shine into the hearts of many of His children, and bring in blessed reality and experience the wondrous Gift of Love of which they tell--the Life and the Joy of the Holy Ghost, as He brings nigh and glorifies within them that Jesus whom hitherto they have only known at a distance, high above them.

I must confess to having had still another wish. I have strong fears-I desire to say it in deep humility-that in the theology of our Churches the Teaching and Leading of the Spirit of Truth, the anointing which alone teacheth all things, has not practical recognition which a Holy God demands, which our Savior meant Him to have. In everything that concerns the Word of God, and the church of Christ, and the work of Saving Love to be done on the earth in the name of Christ, it was meant that the Holy Spirit should have the same and supreme place of honor that He had in the Church of the Acts of the Apostles. If the leaders of our church-thought and church-councils, our professors of theology and our commentators, if our ministers and students, our religious writers and workers, were all fully conscious of this fact, surely the signs of that honour given and accepted, marks of His Holy Presence would be clearer, His mighty works more manifest. I trust it has not been presumptuous in me to hope that what has been written may help to remind even our Masters in Israel of what is so easily overlooked , that the first, the indispensable requirement for what is really to bear fruit for eternity is, that it be full of the power of the Eternal Spirit.

I am well aware that it is expected of what asks the attention of our men of mind and culture, our "scientific theologians, that it shall bear such marks of scholarship, of force of thought and power of expression, as I cannot dare to lay claim to. And yet I venture to ask any of these honored brethren under whose eyes these lines may come, to regard the book, if in no other aspect, at least as the echo of a cry for light rising from ten thousand hearts, as the statement of questions for the solution of which many are longing. There is a deep feeling abroad that the Scripture ideal, that Christ's own promise of what the Church should be, and its actual state, do not correspond.

Of all questions in theology there is none that leads us more deeply into the glory of God, or that is of more intense vital and practical importance for daily life, than that which deals with what is the consummation and culmination of the Revelation of God and the work of Redemption: in what way and to what extent God's Holy Spirit can dwell in, can fill, can make into a holy and beautiful temple of God, the heart of His child, with Christ reigning there, as an Ever-present and Almighty Savior. It is the question in theology of which the solution, if it were sought and found in the presence and teaching of the Spirit Himself, would transform all our theology into that knowledge of God which is eternal life.

Of theology, in every possible shape, we have no lack. But it is as if, with all our writing, and preaching, and working, there is something wanting. Is not the power from on high the one thing we lack ? May it not be that, with all our love for Christ and labor for His cause, we have not made the chief object of our desire what was the chief object of His heart when He ascended the throne--have

His disciples as a company of men waiting the clothing with the power of the Holy Ghost, that in that power of the felt presence of their Lord they might testify of Him? May God raise from among our theologians many who shall give their lives to secure for God's Holy Spirit His recognition in the lives of believers, in the ministry try of the word by tongue and pen, in all the work done in His Church.

I have noticed with deep interest a call to union in prayer, in the first place, 'that Christian life and teaching may be increasingly subject to the Holy Ghost.' I believe that one of the first blessings of this united prayer will be to direct attention to the reason why such prayer is not more evidently answered, and to the true preparation for receiving an abundant answer. In my reading in connection with this subject, in my observation of the lives of believers, and in my personal experience, I have been very deeply impressed with one thought. It is, that our prayer for the mighty working of the Holy Spirit through us and around us can only be powerfully answered as His indwelling in every believer is more clearly acknowledged and lived out. We have the Holy Spirit within us: only he who is faithful in the lesser will receive the greater. 'As we first yield ourselves to be led by the Spirit, to confess His presence in us; as believers rise to realize and accept His guidance in all their daily life; will our God be willing to entrust to us larger measures of His mighty workings. If we give ourselves entirely into His power, as our life, ruling within us, He will give Himself to us in taking a more complete possession, to work through us.

If there is one thing I desire, it is that the Lord may use what I have written to make clear and impress this one truth: it is as an Indwelling Life that the Holy Spirit must be known. In a living, adoring faith, the Indwelling must be accepted and treasured, until it become part of the consciousness of the new man: The Holy Spirit possesses me. In this faith the whole life, even to the least things, must be surrendered to His leading, while all that is of the flesh or self is crucified and put to death. If in this faith we wait on God for His Divine leading and working, placing ourselves entirely at His disposal our prayer cannot remain unheard; there will be operations and manifestations of the Spirit's power in the Church and the world such as we could not dare to hope. The Holy Spirit only demands vessels entirely set apart to Him. He will delight to manifest the glory of Christ our Lord.

I commit each beloved fellow-believer to the teaching of the Holy Spirit. May we all, as we study His work, be partakers of the anointing which teacheth all things.

ANDREW MURRAY.

WELLINGTON, CAPE OF GOOD HOPE 15th August 1888.

Chapter 1
A New Spirit, and God's Spirit.

A new heart will I give you, and a new spirit will I put within you. And I will put my Spirit within you.' Ezekiel 36:26, 27.

GOD has revealed Himself in two great dispensations. In the Old we have the, time of promise and preparation, in the New that of fulfillment and possession.' In harmony with the difference of the two dispensations, there is a two fold working of God's Spirit. In the Old Testament we have the Spirit of God coming upon men, and working on them in special times and ways, working from above and without, inwards. In the New we have the Holy Spirit entering them and dwelling within them, working from within, outwards and upwards. In the former we have the Spirit of God as the Almighty and Holy One; in the latter we have the Spirit of the Father of Jesus Christ.

The difference between the twofold, operation of the Holy Spirit is not to be regarded as if, with the closing of the Old Testament, the former ceased,and there was in the New no more of the work of preparation. By no means. Just as there were in the Old blessed anticipations of the indwelling of God's Spirit, so now in the New Testament the twofold working still continues. According to the lack of knowledge, or of faith, or - of faithfulness, a believer may even in these days get little beyond the Old Testament measure of the Spirit's working. The indwelling Spirit has indeed been given to every child of God, and yet he may experience little beyond the first half of the promise, the new spirit given us in regeneration, and know almost nothing of God's own Spirit, as a living person put within us. The Spirit's work in convincing of sin and of righteousness, in His leading to repentance and faith and the new life, is but the preparatory work. The distinctive glory of the dispensation of the Spirit is His Divine personal indwelling in the heart of the believer, there to reveal the Father and the Son. It is only as Christians understand and remember this, that they will be able to claim the full blessing prepared for them in Christ Jesus.

In the words of Ezekiel we find, in the one promise, this twofold blessing God bestows through His Spirit very strikingly set forth. The first is, 'I will put within you a new spirit,' that is, man's own spirit is to be renewed and quickened by the work of God's Spirit. When this has been done, then there is the second blessing, ' I will put my Spirit within you,' to dwell in that new spirit, Where God is to dwell, He must have a habitation. With Adam He had to create a body before He could breathe the spirit of life into him. In Israel the tabernacle and the temple had to be built and completed before God could come down and take possession. And just so a new heart is given, and a new spirit put within us, as the indispensable condition of God's own Spirit being given to dwell within us. The difference is the same we find in David's prayer. First, 'Create in me a clean heart, 0 God ! and renew a right spirit within me;' then, 'Take not Thy Holy Spirit from me.' Or what is indicated in the words, 'That which is born of the spirit is spirit :' there is the Divine Spirit begetting, and the new spirit begotten by Him. So the two are also distinguished, 'God's Spirit beareth witness with our spirits that we are the children of God! Our spirit is the renewed regenerate spirit; dwelling in this, and yet to be distinguished from it, is God's Holy Spirit, witnessing in, with, and through it.'

The importance of recognizing this distinction can easily be perceived. We shall then be able to understand the true relation between regeneration and the indwelling of the Spirit. The former is that work of the Holy Spirit, by which He convinces us of sin, leads to repentance and faith in Christ, and imparts a new nature. Through the Spirit God thus fulfills the promise, "I will put a new spirit within you.' The believer is now a child of God, a temple ready for the Spirit to dwelling. Where faith claims it, the second half of the promise is fulfilled as surely as the first. As long now as the believer only looks at regeneration, and the renewal wrought in his spirit, he will not come to the life of joy and strength which is meant for him. But when he accepts God's promise that there is something better than even the new nature, than the inner temple, that there is the Spirit of the Father and the Son to dwell within him, there opens up a wonderful prospect of holiness and blessedness. It becomes his one great desire to know this Holy Spirit aright, how He works and what He asks, to know how he may to the full experience His indwelling, and that revelation of the Son of God within us which it is His work to bestow.

The question will be asked, How these two parts of the Divine promise are fulfilled ? simultaneously or successively ? The answer is very simple: From God's side the twofold gift is simultaneous. The Spirit is not divided: in giving the Spirit, God gives Himself and all He is. So it was on the day of Pentecost. The three thousand received the new spirit, with repentance and faith, and then, when they had been baptized, the Indwelling Spirit, as God's seal to their faith, on one day. Through the word of disciples, the Spirit, which had come upon them, wrought mightily on the multitude, changing disposition and heart and spirit. When, in the power of this new spirit working in them, they had believed and confessed, they received the baptism of Holy Spirit to abide in them. And so still in times when the Spirit of God moves mightily, and the Church is living in the power of the Spirit, the children which are begotten of her receive from the first beginnings of their Christian life the distinct conscious sealing and indwelling of the Spirit. And yet we have indications in Scripture that there may be circumstances, dependent either on the enduement of the preacher or the faith of the bears in which the two halves of the promise are not so closely linked. So it was with the believers in Samaria converted under Philip's preaching; and so too with the converts Paul met at Ephesus. In their case was repeated the experience of the apostles themselves. We regard them as regenerate men before our Lord's death ; it was only at Pentecost that the promise was fulfilled, 'He shall be in you!' What was seen in them, just as in the Old and New Testaments,-the grace of the Spirit divided into two separate manifestations,-may still take place in our day. When, the standard of spiritual life in a Church is sickly and low, when neither in the preaching of the word nor in the testimony of believers, the glorious truth of an Indwelling Spirit is distinctly proclaimed, we must not wonder if, even where God gives His Spirit, He be known and experienced only as the Spirit of regeneration. His Indwelling Presence will remain a mystery. In the gift of God, the Spirit of Christ in all His fullness is bestowed once for all as an Indwelling Spirit; but He is received and possessed only as far as the faith of the believer reaches.

It is generally admitted in the Church that the Holy Spirit has - not the recognition which becomes Him as being the equal of the Father and the Son, the Divine Person through whom alone the Father and the Son can be truly possessed and known, in whom alone the Church has her beauty and her blessedness. In the Reformation, of blessed memory, the Gospel of Christ had to be vindicated from the terrible misapprehension which makes man's righteousness the ground of his acceptance, and the freeness of Divine grace had to be maintained. To the ages that followed was committed the trust of building on that foundation, and developing what the riches of grace would do for the believer through the indwelling of the Spirit of Jesus. The Church rested too content in what it had received, and the teaching of all that the Holy Spirit will be to each believer in His guiding, sanctifying, strengthening power, has never yet taken the place it ought to have in our evangelical teaching and living.

And there is many an earnest Christian who will in the confession lately made by a young believer of intelligence: I think I understand the work of the Father and the Son, and rejoice in them, but I hardly see the place the Spirit has. Let us unite with all who are pleading that God in power may grant mighty Spirit workings in His Church, that each child of God may prove that in him the double promise is fulfilled: I will give a new spirit within you, and I will give my Spirit within you. Let us pray that we may so apprehend the wonderful blessing of the Indwelling Spirit, as to turn inward and have our whole inmost being opened up for this, the full revelation of the Father's love and the grace of Jesus.

'Within you ! ' Within you ! This twice-repeated word of our text is one of the keywords of the 'New Covenant. ' I will put my law in their inward parts, 'and in their heart will I write it.' I will put my fear in their hearts, that they shall not depart from me.' God created man's heart for His dwelling. Sin entered, and defiled it. Four thousand years God's Spirit strove and wrought to regain possession. In the Incarnation and Atonement of Christ the Redemption was accomplished, and the kingdom of God established. Jesus could say, 'The kingdom of God is come unto you;' 'the kingdom of God is within you.' It is within we must look for the fulfillment of the New Covenant, the Covenant not of ordinances but of life: in the power of an endless life the law and the fear of God are to be given in our heart: the Spirit of Christ Himself is to be within us as the power of our life. Not only on Calvary, or in the resurrection, or on the throne, is the glory of Christ the Conqueror to be seen,-but in our heart: within us, within us is to be the true display of the reality and the glory of His Redemption. Within us, in our inmost parts, is the hidden sanctuary where is the ark of the Covenant, sprinkled with the Blood, and containing the Law written in an ever-living writing by the Indwelling Spirit, and where, through the Spirit, the Father and the Son now come to dwell.

O my God! I do thank Thee for this double blessing. I thank Thee for that wonderful holy temple Thou hast built up in me for Thyself-a new spirit given within me. And I thank Thee for that still more wonderful Holy Presence, Thine Own Spirit, to dwell within me, and there reveal the Father and the Son.

O my God! I do pray Thee to open mine eyes for this the mystery of Thy love. Let Thy words, within you,' bow me low in trembling fear before Thy condescension, and may my one desire be to have my spirit indeed the worthy dwelling of Thy Spirit. Let them lift me up in holy trust and expectation, to look for and claim all that Thy promise means.

O my Father!, I thank Thee that Thy Spirit doth dwell in me. I pray Thee, let His indwelling :be in power, in the living fellowship with Thyself, in the growing experience of His renewing power, in the ever fresh anointing that witnesses to His Presence, and the indwelling of my Glorified Lord Jesus. May my daily walk be in the deep reverence of His Holy Presence within me, and the glad experience of all He works. Amen.

Chapter 2
The Baptism of the Spirit

'John bare witness, saying, He that sent me to baptize with water, He said unto me, Upon Whomsoever thou shalt see the, Spirit descending, and abiding on Him the same is He that baptizeth with the Holy Spirit.' John 1:33

There were two things that John the Baptist preached concerning the person of Christ, The one was, that He was the Lamb of God that taketh away the sin of the world The other, that He would baptize His disciples with the Holy Ghost and with fire. The Blood of the Lamb, and the Baptism of the Spirit were the two central truths of his creed and his preaching. They are,indeed, inseparable: the Church cannot do her work in power, nor can her exalted Lord be glorified in her, except as the Blood as the foundation-stone, and the Spirit as the corner-stone, are fully preached.

This has not at all times been done even among those who heartily accept Scripture as their guide. The preaching of the Lamb of God, of His suffering and atonement, of pardon and peace through Him, is more easily apprehended by the understanding of man, and can more speedily influence his feelings, than the more inward spiritual truth of the baptism, and indwelling, and guidance of the Holy Spirit. The pouring out of the blood took place upon earth, it was something visible and outward, and, in virtue of the types, not unintelligible. The pouring out of the Spirit was in heaven, a Divine and hidden mystery. The shedding of the blood was for the ungodly and rebellious; the gift of the Spirit, for the loving and obedient disciple. It is no wonder, when the life of the Church is not in very intense devotion to her Lord, that the preaching and the faith of the Baptism of the Spirit should find less entrance than that of redemption and forgiveness.

And yet God would not have it so. The Old Testament Promise had spoken of God's Spirit within us. The forerunner at once took up the strain,and did not preach the Atoning Lamb without telling whereunto it was that we were to be redeemed, and how God's high purpose was to be fulfilled in us. Sin was not only guilt and condemnation; it was defilement and death. It had incurred not only the loss of God's favor it had made us unfit for the Divine fellowship. And without this the wonderful love that had created man could not be content. God wanted really to have us for Himself, -our hearts and affections, yea, our inmost personality, our very self, a home for His love to rest in, a temple for His worship. The preaching of John included both the beginning and the end of redemption: the blood of the Lamb was to cleanse God's Temple and restore His Throne within the heart; nothing less than the Baptism and Indwelling of the Spirit could satisfy the heart of either God or man.

Of what that Baptism of the Spirit meant, Jesus Himself was to be the type : He would only give what He Himself had received: because the Spirit abode on Him, He could baptize with the Spirit. And what did the Spirit descending and abiding on Him mean? He had been begotten of the Holy Spirit; in the power of the Spirit He had grown up a holy child and youth, had entered manhood free from sin, and had now come to John to give Himself to fulfill all righteousness in submitting to the baptism of repentance. And now, as the reward of His obedience, as the Father's seal of approval on His having thus far yielded to the control of the Spirit, He receives a new communication of the Power of the Heavenly Life. Beyond what -He had yet experienced, the Father's conscious indwelling presence and power takes possession of Him, and fits Him for His work. The leading and the power of the Spirit become His more consciously (Luke 4: 1, 14, 22) than before; He is now anointed with the Holy Ghost and with power.

But though now baptized Himself, He cannot yet baptize others. He must first, in the power of His baptism, meet temptation and overcome it; must learn obedience and suffer, yea, through the Eternal Spirit, offer Himself a sacrifice unto God and His will,--then only would He afresh receive the Holy Spirit as the reward of obedience (Acts 2: 33), with the power to baptize all who belong to Him.

What we see in Jesus teaches us what the baptism of the Spirit is. It is not. that grace by which we turn to God, become regenerate, and seek to live as God's children. When Jesus reminded His disciples (Acts 1: 4) of John's prophecy, they were already partakers of this grace. Their baptism with the Spirit meant something more. It was to be to them the conscious presence of their glorified Lord, come back from heaven to dwell in their hearts, their participation in the power of His new Life. It was to them a baptism of joy and power in their living fellowship with Jesus on the Throne of Glory. All that they were further to receive of wisdom, and courage, and holiness, had its root in this: what the Spirit had been to Jesus, when He was baptized, as the living bond with the Father's Power and Presence, He was to be to them: through Him, the Son was to manifest Himself, and Father and Son were to make their abode with them.

'Upon whom thou shalt see the Spirit descending, and abiding upon Him, the same is He that baptizeth with the Holy Spirit.' This word comes to us as well as to John. To know what the baptism of the Spirit means, how and from whom we are to receive it we must see the One upon whom the Spirit descended and abode. We must see Jesus baptized with the Holy Ghost. We must try to understand how He needed it, how He was prepared for it, how He yielded to it, how in its power He died His death, and was raised again. What Jesus has to give us, He first received and personally appropriated for Himself ; what He received and won for Himself is all for us: He will make it our very own. Upon whom we see the Spirit abiding, He baptizeth with the Spirit.

In regard to this baptism of the Spirit there are questions that we may not find it easy to answer, and to which all will not give the same answer. Was the outpouring of the Spirit at Pentecost the complete fulfillment of the promise, and is that the only baptism of the Spirit, given once for all to the newborn Church ? Or is not the coming of the Holy Spirit on the disciples in the fourth of Acts, on the Samaritans (Acts 8), on the heathen in the house of Cornelius (Acts 10.), and on the twelve disciples at Ephesus (Acts 19), also to be regarded as separate fulfilments of the words, 'He shall baptize with the Holy Ghost'? Is the sealing of the Spirit given to each believer in regeneration to be counted by him as his baptism of the Spirit ? Or is it, as some say, a distinct, definite blessing to be received later on ? Is it a blessing given only once, or can it be repeated and renewed ? -In the course of our study we shall find light in God's word that may help us to a solution of difficulties like these. But it is of great consequence that at the outset we should not allow ourselves to be occupied with points as these, which are after all of minor importance, but fix our whole hearts on the great spiritual lessons that God would have us learn from the preaching of the Baptism of the Holy Ghost. These are specially two.

The one is, that this baptism of the Holy Spirit is the crown and glory of Jesus' work, that we need it, and must know that we have it, if we are to live the true Christian life. We need it. The Holy Jesus needed it. Christ's loving, obedient disciples needed it. It is something more than the working of the Spirit in regeneration. It is the Personal Spirit of Christ making Him present within us, always abiding in the heart in the power of His glorified nature, as He is exalted above every enemy. It is the Spirit of the Life of Christ Jesus making us free from the law of sin and death, and bringing us, as a personal experience, into the liberty from sin to which Christ redeemed us, but which to so many regenerate is only a blessing registered, on their behalf, but not possessed or enjoyed. It is the enduement with power to fill us with boldness in presence of every danger, and give the victory over the world and every enemy. It is the fulfillment of what

God meant in His promise - I will dwell in them, and walk in them. Let us ask the Father to reveal to us all that His love meant for us, until our souls are filled with the glory of the thought: He baptizeth with the Holy Spirit.

And then there is the other lesson: It is Jesus who thus baptizeth. Whether we look upon this baptism as something we already have, and of which we only want a fuller apprehension, or something we still must receive, in this all agree : it is only in the fellowship of Jesus, in faithful attachment and obedience to Him, that a baptized life can be received or maintained or renewed. 'He that believeth in me,' Jesus, said, 'out of his belly shall flow rivers of living water.' The one thing we need is living faith in the indwelling Jesus: the living water will surely and freely flow. Faith is the instinct of the new nature, by which it recognizes and receives its Divine food and drink. In the power of the Spirit who dwells in every believer, let us trust Jesus, who fills with the Spirit, and cling to Him in love and obedience. It is He who baptizes: in contact with Him, in devotion to Him, in the confidence that He has given and will give Himself wholly to us, let us look to Him for nothing less than all that the baptism of the Spirit can imply.

In doing so let us specially remember one thing: only he that is faithful in the least will be made ruler over much. Be very faithful to what thou already hast and knowest of the Spirit's working. Regard thyself with deep reverence as God's holy temple. Wait for and listen to the gentlest whispering of God's Spirit within thee. Listen especially to the conscience, which has been cleansed in the blood. Keep that conscience very clean by simple childlike obedience. In thy heart there may be much involuntary sin, with which thou feelest thyself powerless. Humble thyself deeply for thy inbred corruption, strengthened as it has been by actual sin. Let every rising, of such sin be cleansed in the blood.

But in regard to thy voluntary actions say, day by day, to thy Lord Jesus, that everything thou knowest to be pleasing to Him thou wilt do. Yield to the reproofs of conscience when thou failest; but come again, have hope in God, and renew the vow: What I know God wants me to do, I will do. Ask humbly every morning, and wait, for guidance in thy path; the Spirit's voice will become better known, and His strength will be felt. Jesus had His disciples three years in His baptism class, and then the blessing came. Be His loving, obedient disciple, and believe in Him on whom the Spirit abode, and who is full of the Spirit, and thou too shalt be prepared for the fullness of the blessing of the baptism of the Spirit.

Blessed Lord Jesus! with my whole heart I worship Thee, as exalted on the Throne to baptize with the Holy Ghost. Oh! reveal Thyself to me in this Thy glory, that I may rightly know what I may expect from Thee.

I bless Thee that in Thyself I have seen what the preparation is for receiving the Holy Spirit in His fullness. During Thy life of preparation in Nazareth for

Thy work, O my Lord, the Spirit was always in Thee. And yet when Thou hadst surrendered Thyself to fulfill all righteousness, and to enter into fellowship with the sinners Thou camest to save, in partaking of their baptism, Thou didst receive from the Father a new inflowing of His Holy Spirit. It was to Thee the seal of His love, the revelation of His indwelling, the power for His service. And now Thou, on whom we see the Spirit descend and abide, doest for us what the Father did for Thee.

My Holy Lord I bless Thee that the Holy Spirit is in me too. But, oh I beseech Thee, give me yet the full, the overflowing measure Thou hast promised. Let Him be to me the full unceasing revelation of Thy presence in my heart, as glorious and as mighty as on the Throne of Heaven. 0 my 'Lord Jesus! baptize me, fill me with the Holy Spirit. Amen.

Chapter 3
Worship in the Spirit

'The hour cometh, and now is, when the true worshipers shall worship the Father in Spirit and in truth; for such doth the Father seek to be His worshipers. God is a Spirit, and they that worship Him must worship Him in Spirit and in truth.' John 4:23, 24.

'We are the circumcision, who worship by the Spirit of God and glory in Christ Jesus, and have no confidence in the flesh. Philippians 3:3.

To worship is man's highest glory. He was created for fellowship with God: of that fellowship worship is the sublimest expression. All the exercises of the religious life meditation and prayer, love and faith, surrender and obedience,all culminate in worship. Recognizing what God is in His holiness, His glory, and His love, realizing what I am as a sinful creature, and as the Father's redeemed child, in worship I gather up my whole being and present myself to my God, to offer Him the adoration and the glory which is His due. The truest and fullest and nearest approach to God is worship. Every sentiment and every service of the religious life is included in it: to worship is man's highest destiny, because in it God is all.

Jesus tells us that with His coming a new worship would commence. All that heathen or Samaritans had called worship, all even that the Jews had known of worship in accordance with the provisional revelation of God's law, would make way for something entirely and distinctively new--the worship in Spirit and in Truth. This is the worship He was to inaugurate by the giving of the Holy Spirit. This is the worship which now alone is well pleasing to the Father. It is for this worship specially that we have received the Holy Spirit. Let us, at the very commencement of our study of the work of the Spirit, take in the blessed thought that the great object for which the Holy Spirit is within us is, that we worship in spirit and in truth. 'Such doth the Father seek to be His worshipers,'-for this He sent forth His Son and His Spirit.

In Spirit. When God created man a living soul, that soul, as the seat and organ of his personality and consciousness, was linked, on the one side, through the body, with the outer visible world, on the other side, through the spirit, with the unseen and the Divine. The soul had to decide whether it would yield itself to the spirit, by it to be linked with God and His will, or to the body and the solicitations of the visible. In the fall, the soul refused the rule of the spirit, and became the slave of the body with its appetites. Man became flesh; the spirit lost its destined place of rule, and became little more than a dormant power; it was now no longer the ruling principle, but a struggling captive. And the spirit now stands in opposition to the flesh, the name for the life of soul and body together, in their subjection to sin.

When speaking of the unregenerate man in contrast with the spiritual (1 Cor. 2:14), Paul calls him psychical, soulish, or animal, having only the natural life. The life of the soul comprehends all our moral and intellectual faculties, as they may even be directed towards the things of God, apart from the renewal of the Divine Spirit. Because the soul is under the power of the flesh, man is spoken of as having become flesh, as being flesh. As the body consists of flesh and bone, and the flesh is that part of it which is specially endowed with sensitiveness, and through which we receive our sensations from the outer world, the flesh denotes human nature, as it has become subject to the world of sense. And because the whole soul has thus come under the power of the flesh, the Scripture speaks of all the attributes of the soul as belonging to the flesh, and being under its power. So it contrasts, in reference to religion and worship, the two principles from which they may proceed. There is a fleshly wisdom and a spiritual wisdom (1 Cor.2: 12 ; Col. 1: 9). There is a service of God trusting in the flesh and glorying in the flesh, and a service of God by the spirit (Phil. 3:3, 4; Gal. 6: 13).

There is a fleshly mind and a spiritual mind (Col.2: 18, 1: 9). There is a will of the flesh, and a will which is of God working by His Spirit (John 1:13 ; Phil. 2:13). There is a worship which is a satisfying of the flesh, because it is in the power of what flesh can do (Col.2: 18, 23), and a worship of God which is in the Spirit. It is this worship Jesus came to make possible, and to realize in us, by giving a new spirit in our inmost part, and then, within that, God's Holy Spirit.

'In Spirit and in Truth.' Such a worship in Spirit is worship in Truth. Just as the words in Spirit do not mean internal as contrasted with external observances, but Spiritual, in-wrought by God's Spirit, as opposed to what man's natural power can effect, so the words in Truth do not mean hearty, sincere, upright. In all the worship of the Old Testament saints, they knew that God sought Truth in the inward parts; they sought Him with their whole hearts, and most uprightly,and yet they attained not to that worship in Spirit and Truth, which Jesus brought us when He rent the veil of the flesh. Truth here means the substance, the reality, the actual possession of all that the worship of God implies, both in what it demands and what it promises. John speaks of Jesus as 'the Only Begotten of the Father, full of grace and truth.' And he adds, 'For the Law was given by Moses ; grace and truth came by Jesus Christ.' If we take truth as opposed to falsehood, the law of Moses was just as true as the Gospel of Jesus; they both came from God. But if we understand what it means, that the law gave only a shadow of ' good things to come, and that Christ brought us the things themselves, their very substance, we see how He was full of truth, because He was Himself the Truth, the reality, the very Life and Love and Power of God imparting itself to us. We then also see how it is only a worship in Spirit that can be a worship in Truth, in the actual enjoyment of that Divine Power, which is Christ's own life and fellowship with the Father, revealed and maintained within us by the Holy Spirit.

'The true worshipers worship the Father in Spirit and in Truth.' All worshipers are not true worshipers. There may be a great deal of earnest honest worship without its being worship in Spirit and in Truth. The mind may be intensely occupied, the feelings may be deeply moved, the will may be mightily roused, while yet there is but little of the Spiritual Worship which stands in the Truth of God. There may be great attachment to Bible truth, and yet through the predominating activity of that which cometh not from God's working but from man's effort, it may not be the Christ--given, Spirit-breathed worship which God seeks. There must be accordance, harmony, unity between God, who is a Spirit, and the worshipers drawing near in the Spirit. Such doth the Father seek to worship Him. The Infinite, Perfect, Holy Spirit which God the Father is, must have some reflection in the spirit which is in the child.

And this can only be as the Spirit of God dwells in us. If we would strive to become such worshipers in Spirit and in Truth,-true worshipers,-the first thing we need is a sense of the danger in which we are from the Flesh and its worship. As believers we have in us a double nature-flesh and spirit. The one is the natural part which is ever ready to intrude itself, and to undertake the doing of what is needed in the Worship of God. The other is the Spiritual part, which may still be very weak, and which possibly we do not yet know how to give its full sway. Our mind may delight in the study of God's Word, our feelings may be moved by the wonderful thoughts there revealed, our will may--we see this in Rom.7: 22--delight in the law of God after the inward man, and we may yet be impotent to do that law, to render the obedience and worship we see and approve.

We need the Holy Spirit's indwelling for life and worship alike. And to receive this we need first of all to have the flesh silenced. 'Be silent, all flesh, before the Lord.' 'Let no flesh glory in His presence.' To Peter had already been revealed by the Father that Jesus was the Christ, and yet in his thoughts of the cross he savored not, his mind was not according to, the things of God, but the things of men. Our own thoughts of Divine things, our own efforts to waken or work the right feelings must be given up, our own power to worship must be brought down and laid low, and every approach to God must take place under a very distinct and very quiet surrender to the Holy Spirit. And as we learn how impossible it is at our will any moment to ensure the Spirit's working, we shall learn that if we would worship in the Spirit we must walk in the Spirit. 'Ye are not in the flesh but in the Spirit, if so be the Spirit of God dwelleth in you.' As the Spirit dwells and rules in me, I am in the Spirit, and can worship in the Spirit.

'The hour cometh, and now is, when the true worshipers shall worship the Father in Spirit and in Truth. For such doth the Father seek to be His worshipers.' Yes, the Father seeks such worshipers, and what He seeks He finds, because He Himself works it. That we might be such worshipers, He sent His own Son to seek and to save the lost; to save us with this salvation, that we should become His true worshipers, who enter in through the rent veil of the flesh, and worship Him in the Spirit. And then He sent the Spirit of His Son, the Spirit of Christ, to be in us the Truth and Reality of what Christ had been, His actual presence, to communicate within us the very life that Christ had lived. Blessed be God! the hour has come, and is now, we are living in it this very moment, that the true worshipers shall worship the Father in Spirit and in Truth. Let us believe it; the Spirit has been given, and dwells within us, for this one reason, because the Father seeks such worshipers. Let us rejoice in the confidence that we can attain to it, we can be true worshipers, because the Holy Spirit has been given.

Let us realize in holy fear and awe that He dwells within us. Let us humbly, in the silence of the flesh, yield ourselves to His leading and teaching. Let us wait in faith before God for His workings. And let us practice this worship. Let every new insight into what the work of the Spirit means, every exercise of faith in His indwelling or experience of His working, terminate in this as its highest glory: the adoring worship of the Father, the giving Him the Praise, the Thanks, the Honor, and Love which are His alone.

O God ! Thou art a Spirit, and they that worship Thee must worship Thee in Spirit and in Truth. Blessed be Thy name! Thou didst send forth Thine Own Son to redeem and prepare us for the worship in the Spirit; and Thou didst send forth Thy Spirit to dwell in us and fit us for it. And now we have access to the Father, as through the Son, so in the Spirit.

Most Holy God! we confess with shame how much our worship has been in the power and the will of the flesh. By this we have dishonored Thee, and grieved Thy Spirit, and brought infinite loss to our own souls. 0 God! forgive and save us from this sin. Teach us, we pray Thee, never, never to attempt to worship Thee but in Spirit and in Truth.

Our Father ! Thy Holy Spirit dwells in us. We beseech Thee, according to the riches of Thy glory, to strengthen us with might by Him, that our inner man may indeed be a spiritual temple, where spiritual sacrifices are unceasingly offered. And teach us the blessed art, as often as we enter Thy presence, of yielding self and the flesh to the death, and waiting for and trusting the Spirit who is in us, to work in us a worship, a faith and love, acceptable to Thee through Christ Jesus. And, oh! that throughout the universal Church, a worship in Spirit and in Truth may be sought after, and attained, and rendered to Thee day by day. We ask it in the name of Jesus. Amen.

Chapter 4
The Spirit and the Word

'It is the Spirit that quickeneth ; the flesh profiteth nothing; the words that I have spoken unto you are Spirit and are life. Lord, to whom shall we go? I Thou hast the words of eternal life.' John 6:63, 68.

'The letter killeth, but the Spirit giveth life.' 2 Corinthains 3:6.

Our Blessed Lord had been speaking of Himself as the Bread of Life, and of His flesh and blood as the meat and drink of eternal Life. To many of His disciples it was a hard saying, which they could not understand. Jesus tells them that it is only when the Holy Spirit is come, and they have Him, that His words will become clear to them. He says, 'It is the Spirit that quickeneth ; the flesh profiteth nothing. The words that I have spoken unto you, they are Spirit, and they are Life.'

'It is the Spirit that quickeneth,' in these words and the corresponding ones of Paul, ' the Spirit giveth life,' we have the nearest approach to what may be called a definition of the Spirit. (Comp. 1 Cor. 15: 45, 'a life-giving Spirit.') The Spirit always acts, in the first place, whether in nature or grace, as a Life-giving principle. It is of the deepest importance to keep firm hold on this. His work in the believer, of Sealing, Sanctifying, Enlightening, and Strengthening, is all rooted in this: it is as He is known and honored, and place given to Him, as He is waited on as the Inner Life of the soul, that His other gracious workings can be experienced. These are but the outgrowth of the Life ; it is in the power of the Life within that they can be enjoyed. 'It is the Spirit that quickeneth.'

In contrast to the Spirit our Lord places the flesh. He says, 'the flesh profiteth nothing.' He is not speaking of the flesh as the fountain of sin, but in its religious aspect, as it is the power in which the natural man, or even the believer who does not fully yield to the Spirit, seeks to serve God, or to know and possess Divine things. The futile character of all its efforts our Lord indicates in the words, 'profiteth nothing;' they are not sufficient, they avail not to reach the Spiritual reality, the Divine things themselves. Paul means the same when he contrasts with the Spirit, the letter that killeth. The whole Dispensation of the Law was but a dispensation of the letter and the flesh. Though it had a certain glory, and Israel's privileges were very great, yet, as Paul says, 'Even that which was made glorious had no glory in this respect, by reason of the glory that excelleth.'

Even Christ Himself, as long as He was in the flesh, and until, in the rending of the veil of His flesh, the dispensation of the Spirit took the place of that of the flesh, could not by His words effect in His disciples what He desired. 'It is the Spirit that quickeneth; the flesh profiteth nothing!

Our Lord applies this saying now specially to the words He had just spoken, and the Spiritual truth they contained. ' The words that I have spoken unto you are Spirit and are Life.' He wishes to teach the disciples two things. The one is, that the words are indeed a living seed, with a power of germinating and springing up, asserting their own vitality, revealing their meaning, and proving their Divine Power in those who receive them and keep them abiding in the heart. He wanted them not to be discouraged if they could not at once comprehend them. His words are Spirit and Life; they are not meant for the understanding, but for the Life. Coming in the Power of the Unseen Spirit, higher and deeper than all thought, they enter into the very roots of the Life, they have themselves a Divine Life, working out effectually with a Divine energy the Truth they express into the experience of those who receive them. As a consequence of this their spiritual character--this is the other lesson He wished His disciples to learn--these words of His need a spiritual nature to receive them. Seed needs a congenial soil: there must be life in the soil as well as in the seed. Not into the mind only, nor into the feelings, nor ever, the will alone must the word be taken, but through them into the life. The center of that life is man's spiritual nature, with conscience as its voice ; there the authority of the word must be acknowledged. But even this is not enough: conscience dwells in man as a captive amid powers it cannot control. It is the Spirit that comes from God, the Spirit that Christ came to bring, becoming our life, receiving the word and assimilating it to our life, that will make them to become the Truth and Power in us.

In our study of the work of the Blessed Spirit, we cannot be too careful to get clear and firm hold ,of this blessed truth. It will save us from right-hand and left-hand errors. It will keep us from expecting to enjoy the teaching of the Spirit without the Word, or to master the teaching of the Word without the Spirit.

On the one side, we have the right-hand error, seeking the teaching of the Spirit without the Word. In the Holy Trinity, the Word and the Spirit are ever in each other, one with the Father. It is not otherwise with the God-inspired Words of Scripture. The Holy Spirit has for all ages embodied the thoughts of God in the written word, and lives now for this very purpose in our hearts, there to reveal the power and the meaning of that Word. If you would be full of the Spirit, be full of the Word, If you would have the Divine Life of the Spirit within you grow strong, and acquire power in every part of your nature; let the Word of Christ dwell richly in you. If you would have the Spirit fulfill His office of Remembrancer, calling to mind at the right moment, and applying with Divine accuracy what Jesus has spoken to your need, have the Words of Christ abiding in you. If you would have the Spirit reveal to you the Will of God in each circumstance of life, choosing from apparently conflicting commands or Principles with unerring precision what you must do, and suggesting it as you need, oh ! have the Word living in you, ready for His use. If you would have the Eternal Word as your Light, let the Written Word be transcribed on your heart by the Holy Spirit. 'The Words that I have spoken unto you, they are Spirit and are Life.' Take them and treasure them: it is through them that the Spirit manifests His quickening power.'

On the other side, we have the left-hand and more common error. Think not for one moment that the Word can unfold its Life in thee, except as the Spirit within thee accepts and appropriates it in the inner life. How much of Scripture reading, and Scripture study, and Scripture preaching is there in which the first and main object is to reach the meaning of the Word? Men think that if they know correctly and exactly what it means, there will come as a natural consequence the blessing the Word is meant to bring. This is by no means the case. The Word is a seed. In every seed there is a fleshy part, in which the life is hidden. One may have the most precious and perfect seed in its bodily substance, and yet unless it be exposed in suitable soil to the influence of sun and moisture, the life may never grow up. And so we may hold the words and the doctrines of Scripture most intelligently and earnestly, and yet know little of their life or power. We need to remind ourselves and the Church unceasingly, that the Scriptures which were spoken by holy men of old as they were moved by the Holy Spirit, can only be understood by holy men as they are taught by the same Spirit. The words I have spoken are Spirit and Life;' for the apprehending and partaking of them ' the flesh profiteth nothing : it is the Spirit that quickeneth,' the Spirit of Life within us.

This is one of the awfully solemn lessons which the history of the Jews in the time of Christ teaches us. They were exceeding zealous, as they thought, for God's word and honor, and yet it turned out that all their zeal was for their human interpretation of God's word. Jesus said to them: 'Ye search the Scriptures, because ye think that in them ye have eternal life; and these are they which testify of me: and ye will not come to me that ye may have life.' They did indeed trust to the Scriptures to lead them to eternal life; and yet they never saw that they testified of Christ, and so they would not come to Him. They studied and accepted Scripture in the light and in the power of their human understanding, and not in the light and power of God's Spirit as their life. The feebleness of the life of so many believers who read and know Scripture much has no other cause;they know not that it is the Spirit that quickeneth that the flesh, that the human understanding, however intelligent, however earnest, profiteth nothing. They think that in the Scriptures they have eternal life, but the living Christ, in the power of the Spirit, as their life, they know but little.

What is needed is very simple: the determined refusal to attempt to deal with the written word without the quickening Spirit. Let us never take Scripture into our hand, or mind, or mouth, without realizing the need and the promise of the Spirit. First, in a quiet act of worship, look to God to give and renew the workings of His Spirit within you; then, in a quiet act of faith, yield yourself to the power that dwells in you, and wait on Him, that not the mind alone, but the life in you, may be opened to receive the Word. Let the Holy Spirit be your life. To the Spirit and the Life coming out from within to meet the Word from without as its food, the words of Christ are indeed Spirit and Life.

As we further follow the teaching of our Blessed Lord as to the Spirit, it will become clear to us that, as the Lord's Words are Spirit and Life, so the Spirit must be in us as the Spirit of our Life, Our inmost personal life must be the Spirit of God.

Deeper down than mind, or feeling, or will, the very root of all these, and their animating principle, there must be the Spirit of God. As we seek to go lower down than these, as we see that nothing can reach the Spirit of Life which there is in the words of the Living God, and wait on the Holy Spirit within us, in the unseen depths of the hidden life, to receive and reveal the words in His quickening power, and work them into the very life of our life, we shall know in truth what it means: 'It is the Spirit that quickeneth.' We shall see how divinely right and becoming it is that the words which are Spirit and Life should be met in us by the Spirit and the Life dwelling within, how then alone they will unfold their meaning and impart their substance, and give their divine strength and fullness to the Spirit and the Life already within us.

O my God! again I thank Thee for the wonderful gift of the indwelling Spirit. And I humbly beseech Thee anew that I may indeed know that He is in me, and how glorious the divine work He is carrying on. Teach me specially, I pray Thee, to believe that He is the life and the strength of the growth of the Divine life within me, the pledge and assurance that I can grow up into all my God would have me. As I see this, I shall understand how He, as the Spirit of the Life within me, will make my spirit hunger for the Word as the food of the life, will receive and assimilate it, will indeed make it Life and Power.

Forgive me, my God, that I have so much sought to apprehend Thy words, which are Spirit and Life, in the power of human thought and the fleshly mind. I have been so slow to learn that the flesh profiteth nothing. I do desire to learn it now.

O my Father! give me the Spirit of wisdom, grant me the mighty workings of the Spirit, that I may know how deeply spiritual each word of Thine is, and how spiritual things can only be spiritually discerned. - Teach me in all my intercourse with Thy word to deny the flesh and the fleshly mind, to wait in deep humility and faith for the inward working of the Spirit to quicken the word. May thus all my meditation of Thy Word, all my keeping of it in faith and obedience, be in Spirit and in Truth, in Life and Power. Amen.

Chapter 5
The Glorified Jesus

The Spirit of the glorified Jesus He that believeth on Me, as the Scripture hath said, out of his belly shall flow rivers of living water. But this spake He of the Spirit, which they that believe on Him were to receive for the Spirit was not yet; because Jesus was not yet glorified,' John 7: 37, 38

Our Lord promises here, that those who come unto Him and drink, who believe in Him, will not only never thirst, but will themselves become fountains, whence streams of living water, of life and blessing, will flow forth. In recording the words, John explains that the promise was a prospective one, that would have to wait for its fulfillment till the Spirit should have been poured out. He also gave the double reason for this delay: The Holy Spirit was not yet; because Jesus was not yet glorified. The expression : the Spirit was not yet, has appeared strange, and so the word given has been inserted. But the expression, if accepted as it stands, may guide us into the true understanding of the real significance of the Spirit's not coming until Jesus was glorified.

We have seen that God has given a twofold revelation of Himself, first as, God in the Old Testament, then as Father in the New. We know how the Son, who had from eternity been with the Father, entered upon a new stage of existence when He became flesh. When He returned to Heaven, He was still the same only-begotten Son of God, and yet not altogether the same. For He was now also, as Son of Man, the first-begotten from the dead, clothed with that glorified humanity which He had perfected and sanctified for Himself. And just so the Spirit of God as poured out on Pentecost was indeed something new. Through the Old Testament He was always called the Spirit of God or the Spirit of the Lord; the name of Holy Spirit He did not yet bear as His own proper name.' It is only in connection with the work He has to do in preparing the way for Christ, and a body for Him, that the proper name comes into use (Luke 1: 15, 35). When poured out at Pentecost, He came as the Spirit of the glorified Jesus, the Spirit of the Incarnate, crucified, and exalted Christ, the bearer and communicator to us, not of the life of God as such, but of that life as it had been interwoven into human nature in the person of Christ Jesus. It is in this capacity specially that He bears the name of Holy Spirit, it is as the Indwelling One that God is Holy. And of this Spirit, as He dwelt in Jesus in the flesh, and can dwell in us in the flesh too, it is distinctly and literally true ; the Holy Spirit was not yet. The Spirit of the glorified Jesus, the Son of man become the Son of God He could not be ,until Jesus was glorified.

This thought opens up to us further the reason why it is not the Spirit of God as such, but the Spirit of Jesus, that could be sent to dwell in us. Sin had not only disturbed our relation to God's law, but to God Himself ; with the Divine favour we had lost the Divine life. Christ came not only to deliver man from the law and its curse, but to bring human nature itself again into the fellowship of the Divine life, to make us partakers of the Divine nature. He could do this, not by an exercise of Divine Power on man, but only in the path of a free, moral, and most real human development. In His own person, having become flesh, He had to sanctify the flesh, and make it a meet and willing receptacle for the indwelling of the Spirit of God. Having done this, He had, in accordance with the law that the lower form of life rise to a higher, only through decay and death ,in death both to bear the curse of sin and to give Himself as the seed-corn to bring forth fruit in us. From His nature, as it was glorified in the resurrection and ascension, His Spirit came forth as the Spirit of His human life, glorified into the union with the Divine, to make us partakers of all that He had personally wrought out and acquired, of Himself and His glorified life. In virtue of His atonement, man now had a right and title to the fullness of the Divine Spirit, and to His indwelling, as never before. And in virtue of His having perfected in Himself a new holy human nature on our behalf, He could now communicate what previously had no existence,-a life at once human and Divine. From henceforth the Spirit, just as He was the personal Divine life, could also become the personal life of men. Even as the Spirit is the personal life principle in God Himself, so He can be it in the child of God: the Spirit of God's Son can now be the Spirit that cries in our heart, Abba, Father. Of this Spirit it is most fully true, 'The Spirit was not yet, because Jesus was not yet glorified."

But now, Blessed be God ! Jesus has been glorified ; there is now the Spirit of the glorified Jesus; the promise can now be fulfilled: He that believeth on me, out of him shall flow rivers of living waters. The great transaction which took place when Jesus was glorified is now an eternal reality. When Christ had entered with our human nature, in our flesh, into the Holiest of all, there took place that of which Peter speaks, 'Being by the right hand of God exalted, He received of the Father the promise of the Holy Ghost.'In our place, and on our behalf, as man and the Head of man, He was admitted into the full glory of the Divine, and His human nature constituted the receptacle and the dispenser of the

Divine Spirit. And the Holy Spirit could come down as the Spirit of the God-man --most really the Spirit of God, and yet as truly the spirit of man. He could come down as the Spirit of the glorified Jesus to be in each one who believes in Jesus, the Spirit of His personal life and His personal presence, and at the same time the spirit of the personal life of the believer. Just as in Jesus the perfect union of God and man had been effected and finally completed when He sat down upon the throne, and He so entered on a new, stage of existence, a glory hitherto unknown, so too, now, a new era has commenced in the life and the work of the Spirit. He can now come down to witness of the perfect union of the Divine and the human, and in becoming our life, to make us partakers of it. There is now the Spirit of the glorified Jesus: He hath poured Him forth; we have received Him to stream into us, to stream through us, and to stream forth from us in rivers of blessing.

The glorifying of Jesus and the streaming forth of His Spirit are intimately connected; in vital organic union the two are inseparably linked.. If we would have, not only the Spirit of God, but this Spirit of Christ, which 'was not yet,'but now is, the Spirit of the glorified Jesus, it is specially with the glorified Jesus we must believingly deal. We must not simply rest content with the faith that trusts in the cross and its pardon; we must seek to know the New Life, the Life of Glory and Power Divine in human nature, of which the Spirit of the glorified Jesus is meant to be the Witness and the Bearer. This is the mystery which was hid from ages and generations, but is now made known by the Holy Spirit, Christ in us; how He really can live His Divine life in us who are in the flesh. We have the most intense personal interest in knowing and understanding what it means that Jesus is glorified, that human nature shares the life and glory of God, that the Spirit was not yet, as long as Jesus was not glorified. And that not only because we are one day to see Him in His glory, and to be with Him in it. No, but even now, day by day, we are to live in it. The Holy Spirit is able to be to us just as much as we are willing to have of Him, and of the life of the glorified Lord.

'This spake Jesus of the Spirit, which they that believed on Him were to receive; for the Spirit was not yet; because Jesus was not yet glorified.' God be praised! Jesus has been glorified: there is now the Spirit of the glorified Jesus; we have received Him. In the Old Testament only the unity of God was revealed; when the Spirit was mentioned, it was always as His Spirit, the power by which God was working: in the New was not known on earth as a Person. In the New Testament the Trinity is revealed; with Pentecost - the Holy Spirit descended as a Person to dwell in us. This is the fruit of Jesus' work, that we now have the Personal Presence of the Holy Spirit on earth. Just as in Christ

Jesus, the second Person, the Son, came to reveal the Father, and the Father dwelt and spoke in Him, even so the Spirit, the third Person, comes to reveal the Son, and in Him the Son dwells and works in us. This is the glory wherewith the Father glorified the Son of man, because the Son had glorified Him, that in His Name and through Him, the Holy Spirit descends as a Person to dwell in believers, and to make the glorified Jesus a Present Reality within them. This is it of which Jesus says, that whoso believeth in Him shall never thirst, but shall have rivers of waters flowing out of him. This alone it is that satisfies the soul's thirst, and makes it a fountain to quicken others; the Personal Indwelling of the Holy Spirit, revealing the Presence of the glorified Jesus.

' He that believeth on me, rivers of water shall flow out of him. This spake He of the Spirit.' Here we have once again the, blessed Key of all God's treasures : He that believeth on me .It is the glorified Jesus who baptizes with the Holy Ghost: let us believe in Him. Let each one who longs for the full blessing here promised only believe. Let us believe in Him, that He is indeed glorified, that all He is and does and wishes to do is in the power of a Divine glory.

According to the riches of His glory, God can now work in us. Let us believe that he has given His Holy Spirit, that we have the personal presence of the Spirit on earth and within us. By this faith the glory of Jesus in heaven and the Power of the Spirit in our hearts become inseparably linked. Let us believe that in the fellowship with Jesus the stream will flow ever stronger and fuller, into us and out of us. Yes; let us believe on Jesus. But let us remember : thinking on these things, understanding them, being very sure of them, rejoicing in a fuller insight into them, all this, though needful, is not itself believing.

Faith is surrender: believing is that power of the renewed nature which, forsaking self and dying to it, makes room for the Divine, for God, for the glorified Christ to come and take possession and do His work. Faith in Jesus bows in lowly stillness and poverty of spirit, to realize that self has nothing, and that Another, the unseen Spirit, has now come in to be its leader, its strength, and its life. Faith in Jesus bows in the stillness of a quiet surrender before Him, fully assured that as it waits on Him, He will cause the river to flow.

Blessed Lord Jesus! I do believe, help Thou mine unbelief. Do Thou, the Author and Perfecter of our faith, perfect the work of faith in me too. Teach me, I pray Thee, with a faith that enters the unseen, to realize what Thy glory is, and what my share in it is even now, according to Thy word: The glory which Thou gavest me, I have given them.' Teach me that the Holy Ghost and His power is the glory which Thou givest us, and that Thou wouldst have us show forth Thy glory in rejoicing in His holy presence on earth and His indwelling in us. Teach me above all, my blessed Lord to take and hold these blessed truths in the mind, but with my spirit that is in my inmost parts, to wait on Thee to be filled with Thy Spirit.

O my glorified Lord I do even now bow before Thy glory in humble faith. Let all the life of self and the flesh be abased and perish, as I worship and wait before Thee. Let the Spirit of Glory become my life. Let His Presence break down all trust in self, and make room for Thee. And let my whole life be one of faith in the Son of God, who loved me, and gave Himself for me. Amen.

Chapter 6
The Indwelling Spirit

I will pray the Father, and He shall give you another Comforter, that He may be with you for ever; even the Spirit of truth; whom the world cannot receive; for it beholdeth Him not, neither knoweth Him: ye know Him, for He abideth with you, and shall be in you' John 14:16, 17.

'He shall be in you.' In these simple words our Lord announces that wonderful mystery of the Spirit's indwelling which was to be the fruit and the crown of His redeeming work. It was for this man had been created. It was for this, God's mastery within the heart, the Spirit had striven in vain with men through the past ages. It was for this Jesus had lived and was about to die. Without this the Father's purpose and His own work would fail of their accomplishment. For want of this the intercourse of the Blessed Master with the disciples had effected so little. He had hardly ever ventured to mention it to them, because He knew they would not understand it. But now, on the last night, when it was but a little time, He discloses the Divine Secret that, when He left them, their loss would be compensated by a greater blessing than His bodily presence. Another would come in His stead, to abide with them for ever, and to dwell in them. Dwelling in them, He would prepare them to receive Himself their Lord, and the Father, within them too. 'He shall be in you.'

Our Father has given us a twofold revelation of Himself. In His Son He reveals His Holy Image, and setting him before men invites them to become like Him by receiving Him into their heart and life. In His Spirit He sends forth His Divine Power, to enter into us, and from within prepare us for receiving the Son and the Father. The dispensation of the Spirit is the dispensation of the inner life. In the dispensation of the Word, or the Son, beginning as it did with the creation of man in God's image, continued as it was through all the preparatory stages down to Christ's appearing, in the flesh, all was more external and preparatory. There were at times special and mighty workings of the Spirit; but the indwelling was unknown; man had not yet become an habitation of God in the Spirit. Now first, this was to be attained. The eternal life was to become the very life of man, hiding itself within his very being and consciousness, and clothing itself in the forms of a human will and life. Just as it is through the Spirit that God is what He is; just as in the Father and the Son, the Spirit is the principle in which their personality has its root and consciousness, so this Spirit of the Divine life is now to be in us, in the deepest sense of the word, the principle of our life, the root of our personality too, the very life of our being and consciousness. He is to be one with us in the absoluteness of a Divine immanence, dwelling in us, even as the Father in the Son, and the Son in the Father. Let us bow in holy reverence to worship and adore, and to receive the mighty blessing.

If we would enter into the full understanding and experience of what our Blessed Lord here promises, we must above everything remember that what He speaks of is a Divine indwelling. Wherever God dwells He hides Himself. In nature He hides Himself; most men see Him not there. In meeting His saints of old He mostly hid Himself under some manifestation in human weakness, so that it was often only after He was gone that they said, Surely the Lord is in this place, and I knew it not. 'The Blessed Son came to reveal God, and yet He came as a root out of a dry ground, without form or comeliness; even His own disciples were at times offended at Him. Men always expect the kingdom of God to come with observation ; they know not that it is a hidden mystery, to be received only as, in His own self-revealing power, God makes Himself known in hearts surrendered and prepared for Him. Christians are always ready, when the promise of the Spirit occupies them, to form some conception as to how His leading can be known in their thoughts; how His quickening will affect their feelings; how His sanctifying can be recognized in their will and conduct. They need to be reminded that deeper than mind and feeling and will, deeper than the soul, where these have their seat, in the depths of the spirit that came from God, there comes the Holy Spirit to dwell.

This. indwelling is therefore first of all, and all through, to be recognized by faith. Even when I cannot see the least evidence of His working, I am quietly and reverently to believe that He dwells in me. In that faith I am restfully and trustfully to count upon His working ,and to wait for it. In that faith I must very distinctly deny my own wisdom and strength, and in childlike self-abnegation depend upon Him to work. His first workings may be so feeble and hidden that I can hardly recognize them as coming from Him; they may appear to be nothing more than the voice of conscience, or the familiar sound of some Bible truth. Here is the time for faith to hold fast the Master's promise and the Father's gift, and to trust that the Spirit is within and will guide. In that faith let me continually yield up my whole being to His rule and mastery; let me be faithful to what appears the nearest to His voice; in such faith and such faithfulness my soul will be prepared for knowing His voice better. Out of the hidden depths His power will move to take possession of mind and will, and the indwelling in the hidden recesses of the heart will grow into a being filled with His fullness.

Faith is the one faculty of our spiritual nature by which we can recognize the Divine, in whatever low and unlikely appearances it clothes itself. And if this be true of the Father in His glory as God, and the Son as the manifestation of the Father, how much more must it be true of the Spirit, the unseen Divine life-power come to clothe itself, and hide itself away, within our weakness ? Oh! let us cultivate and exercise much our faith in the Father, whose one gift through the Son is this, the Spirit in our hearts. And in the Son too, whose whole Person and Work and Glory center in the gift of the Indwelling Spirit. And so let out faith grow strong in the unseen, sometimes unfelt Divine Presence of this Mighty Power, this living Person, who has descended into our weakness, and hidden Himself in our littleness, to fit us for becoming the dwelling of the Father and the Son. Let our adoring worship of our glorified Lord ever seek to catch the wondrous answer He gives to every prayer, as the seal of our acceptance, as the promise of deeper knowledge of our God, of closer fellowship and richer blessedness: The Holy Spirit dwelleth in you.

The deep importance of a right apprehension of the indwelling of the Spirit is evident from the place it occupies in our Lord's farewell discourse. In this and the two following chapters, He speaks of the Spirit more directly as Teacher, I as Witness, as representing and glorifying Himself, as convincing the world. At the same time, He connects this, and He says of His and the Father's indwelling, of the union of the Vine and the branches, of the Peace and Joy and Power in Prayer which His disciples would have, with 'that day,' the time of the Spirit's coming. But, before all this, as its one condition and only source, He places the promise, 'the Spirit shall be in, you.' It avails little that we know all that the Spirit can do for us, or that we confess our entire dependence on Him, unless we clearly realize, and place first, what the Master gave the first place ; that it is as the indwelling Spirit alone that He can be our Teacher or our Strength. As the Church, as the believer, accepts our Lord's, ' He shall be in you,' and lives under the control of this faith, our true relation to the Blessed Spirit will be restored. He will take charge and inspire; He will mightily fill and bless the being given up to Him as His abode.

A careful study of the epistles will confirm this, In writing to the Corinthians, Paul had to reprove them for sad and terrible sins, and yet he says to all, including the feeblest and most unfaithful believer, 'Know ye not that the Spirit of God dwelleth in you?' Know ye not that your body is the temple of the Holy Ghost ?' He is sure that if this were believed, if to this truth were given the place

God meant it to have, it would not only be the motive, but the power of a new and holy life. To the backsliding Galatians, he has no mightier plea to address than this : they had received the Spirit by the preaching of faith; God had sent forth the Spirit of His Son into their hearts ; they had their life by the Spirit in them ; if they could but understand and believe this, they would also walk in the Spirit.

It is this teaching the Church of Christ needs in our days. I am deeply persuaded that very few of us realize aright to what extent believers are ignorant of this aspect of the truth concerning the Holy Spirit, or to what an extent this is the cause of their feebleness in holy walk and work. There may be a great deal of praying for the Holy Spirit's working, there may be great correctness in our confession, both in preaching and prayer, of entire and absolute dependence on Him; but unless His personal, continual, Divine indwelling be acknowledged and experienced, we must not be surprised if there be continual failure. The Holy Dove wants his resting place free from all intrusion and disturbance. God wants entire possession of His temple. Jesus wants His home all to Himself. He cannot do His work there, He cannot rule and reveal Himself and His love as He would, unless the whole home, the whole inner being, be possessed and filled by the Holy Spirit. Let us consent to this. As the meaning of the indwelling dawns upon us in its full extent and claims, as we accept it as a Divine reality to be carried out and maintained by nothing less than an Almighty Power, as we bow low in emptiness and surrender, in faith and adoration, to accept the promise and live on it, ' He shall be in you,' the Father will, for Jesus' sake, delight to fulfill it in our experience, and we shall know that the beginning, and the secret, and the power of the life of a true disciple is, the Indwelling Spirit.

Blessed Lord Jesus! my soul doth bless Thee for Thy precious word : The Spirit shall be in you. In deep humility I now once again accept it, and ask Thee to teach me its full and blessed meaning.

I ask for myself and all God's children that we may see how near Thy love would come to us, how entirely and most intimately Thou wouldst give Thyself to us. Nothing can satisfy Thee but to have Thy abode within us, to dwell in us as the life of our life. To this end Thou hast sent forth, from Thy glory, Thy Holy Spirit into our hearts, to be the power that lives and acts in our inmost being, and to give in us the revelation of Thyself. O holy Saviour! bring Thy Church to see this truth that has been so much hid and lost, to experience it, and to bear witness to it in power. May the joyful sound be heard throughout her borders, that every true believer has the indwelling and the leading of Thy Spirit. And teach me, my Lord! the life of faith, that goes out of self, to wait on Thee, as in Thy Spirit Thou dost Thy work within me. May my life from hour to hour be in the holy, humble consciousness: Christ's Spirit dwelleth in me. In humility and silence I bow before this holy mystery, my God ! my Lord Jesus ! Thine own Spirit dwells in me. Amen.

Chapter 7
The Spirit given to the Obedient

If ye love me, ye will keep my commandments: and I will pray the Father, and He shall give you another Comforter, even the Spirit of truth.' John 14:15,16

'The Holy Spirit, whom God hath given to them that obey Him.' Acts 5:32.

The truth which these words express has often suggested the question - How can this be? We need the Spirit to make us obedient; we long for the Spirit's power, just because we mourn so much the disobedience there still is, and desire to be otherwise. And how is this? The Savior claims obedience as the condition of the Father's giving and our receiving the Spirit.

The difficulty will be removed if we remember what we have more than once seen, that there is a twofold manifestation of the Spirit of God, corresponding to the Old and New Testament. In the former, He works as the Spirit of God, preparing the way for the higher revelation of God, as the Father of Jesus Christ. In this way He had worked in Christ's disciples, as the Spirit of conversion and faith. What they were now about to receive was something higher--the Spirit of the glorified Jesus, communicating the power from on high, the experience of His full salvation. And though now, to all believers under the New Testament economy, the Spirit in them is the Spirit of Christ, there is still something that corresponds to the twofold dispensation. Where there is not much knowledge of the Spirit's work, or where His workings in a Church or an individual are but feeble, there even believers will not get beyond the experience of His preparatory workings; though He be in them, they know Him not in His power as the Spirit of the glorified Lord. They have Him in them to make them obedient; it is only as they yield obedience to this His more elementary work, the keeping of Christ's commandments, that they will be promoted to the higher experience of His conscious indwelling, as the Representative and Revealer of Jesus in His glory. 'If ye love me, keep my commandments: and I will pray the Father, and He will send you another Comforter.'

The lesson is one we cannot study too attentively. In Paradise, in the angels of heaven, in God's own Son, by obedience and obedience alone, could the relationship with the Divine Being be maintained, and admission secured to closer experience of His Love and His Life. God's will revealed is the expression of His hidden perfection and being; only in accepting and doing the will, in the entire giving up for the will to possess and use as He pleases, are we fitted for entering the Divine Presence. Was it not thus even with the Son of God? It was when, after a life in holy humility and obedience for thirty years, He had spoken that word of entire consecration, 'It becometh us to fulfill all righteousness,' and given Himself to a baptism for the sins of His people, that He was baptized with the Spirit. The Spirit came because of His obedience. And again, it was after He had learned obedience in suffering, and became obedient to the death of the cross, that He again received the Spirit from the Father (Acts 2: 3 3) to pour out on His disciples. The fullness of the Spirit for His body the Church was the reward of obedience. And this law of the Spirit's coming, as revealed in the Head, holds for every member of the body : obedience is the indispensable condition of the Spirit's indwelling. 'If ye love me, keep my commandments: and the Father will send you the Spirit.'

Christ Jesus had come to prepare the way for the Spirit's coming. Or rather, His outward coming in the flesh was the preparation for His inward coming in the Spirit to fulfill the promise of a Divine indwelling. The outward coming appealed to the soul, with its mind and feeling, and affected these. It was only as Christ in His outward coming was accepted, as He was loved and obeyed, that the Inward and more Intimate revelation would be given. Personal attachment to Jesus, the personal acceptance of Him as Lord and Master to love and obey, was the disciples' preparation for the baptism of the Spirit. And so now , it is as in a tender listening to the voice of conscience, and a faithful effort to keep the commands of Jesus, we prove our love to Him, that the heart will be prepared for the fullness of the Spirit. Our attainments may fall short of our aims, we may have to mourn that what we would we do not--if the Master sees the whole-hearted surrender to His will, and the faithful obedience to what we already have of the leadings of His Spirit, we may be sure that the full gift will not be withheld.

Do not these words suggest to us the two great reasons why the presence and the power of the Spirit in the Church is so feebly realized ? We do not understand that as the obedience of love must precede the fullness of the Spirit, so the fullness of the Spirit must still follow on it. They err who want the fullness of the Spirit before they obey, no less than those who think that obedience is already a sign that the fullness of the Spirit is there. '

Obedience must precede the baptism of the Spirit. John had preached Jesus as the true Baptist--baptizing with the Holy Spirit and with fire. Jesus took His disciples as candidates for this Baptism into a three years' course of training. First of all, attached them to Himself personally. He taught them to forsake all for Him. He called Himself their Master and Lord, and taught them to do what He said. And then in His farewell discourse He time after time spoke of obedience to His commands as the one condition of all further spiritual blessing. It is to be feared that the Church has not given this word Obedience the prominence Christ gave it. Wrong views of the danger of Self-righteousness, of the way in which free Grace is to be exalted, of the power of sin and a needs be of sinning, with the natural reluctance of the flesh to accept a high standard of holiness, have been the causes. While the freedom of grace and the simplicity of faith have been preached, the absolute necessity of obedience and holiness has not been equally insisted on. It has been thought that only those who had the fullness of the Spirit could be obedient. It was not seen that obedience was the lower platform,-that the baptism of the Spirit, the full revelation of the glorified Lord as the Indwelling One in His power to work in us and through us His mighty works, was something higher, the Presence that the obedient should inherit. It was not seen that simple and full allegiance to every dictate of conscience, and every precept of the word, that a ' walk worthy of the Lord to all well-pleasing,' was to be the passport to that full life in the Spirit in which He would witness to the abiding Presence of the Lord in the heart.

As the natural consequence of the neglect of this truth, the companion truth was also forgotten: The obedient must and may look for the fullness of the Spirit. The promise of the special, conscious, active indwelling. of the Spirit to the obedient is a thing to many Christians unknown. The great part of life is spent in mourning over disobedience, over the want of the Spirit's power, and praying for the Spirit to help them to obey, instead of rising in the strength of the Spirit already in them to obedience, as indeed possible and necessary. The thought of the Holy Spirit being specially sent to the obedient to give in them the Presence of Jesus as a continuous reality, that He might do in them the greater works, even as the Father had worked in Him, was hardly thought of. The meaning of the life of Jesus as our example is not understood. How distinctly there was with Him the outward lowly life of trial and obedience in preparation for the hidden spiritual one of Power and Glory! It is this inner life that we are made partakers of in the gift of the Spirit of the glorified Jesus. But in our inner personal participation of that gift we must walk in the way He dedicated for us; as in the crucifixion of the flesh we yield ourselves to God's will, for Him to do in us what He wills, and for us also to do what He wills, we shall experience that God is to be found nowhere but in His will. His will in Christ, accepted and done by us, with the heart in which it is done, is the home of the Holy Spirit. The revelation of the Son in His perfect obedience was the condition of the giving of the Spirit; the acceptance of the Son in love and obedience is the path to the indwelling of the Spirit.

It is this truth which has in these latter years come home with power to the hearts of many in the use of the words full surrender and entire consecration As they understood that the Lord Jesus did indeed claim implicit obedience, that the giving up all to Him and His will was absolutely necessary, and in the power of His grace truly possible, and in the faith of His power did it, they found the entrance to a life of peace and strength formerly unknown. Many are learning, or have to learn, that they do not yet fully know the lesson. They will find that there are applications of this principle beyond what we have conceived. As we see how in the all-pervading power of the Spirit, as we already possess Him, every movement of our life must be brought into allegiance to Jesus, and give ourselves to it in faith, we shall also see that the Spirit of the glorifiied Lord can make Him present and work His mighty works in us and through us, in a way far beyond what we can ask or think. The indwelling of the Holy Spirit was intended by God and Christ to be to the Church more, oh! so much more, than we have yet known., Oh ! shall we not yield ourselves, in a love and obedience that will sacrifice anything for Jesus, that our hearts may be enlarged for the fullness of His blessing prepared for us.

Let us cry to God very earnestly, that He may waken His Church and people to take in this double lesson: A living obedience is indispensable to the full experience of the indwelling; the full experience of the indwelling is what a loving obedience may certainly claim. Let each of us even now say to our Lord that we do love Him, and keep His commandments. In however much feebleness and failure it be, still let us speak it out to Him as the one purpose of our souls; this He will accept. Let us believe in the indwelling of the Spirit as already given to us, when in the obedience of faith we gave ourselves to Him. Let us believe that the full indwelling, with the revelation of Christ within, can be ours. And let us be content with nothing less than the loving, reverent, trembling, but blessed consciousness that we are the Temples of the Living God, because the Spirit of God dwelleth in us.

Blessed Lord Jesus ! with my whole heart do I accept the teaching of these words of Thine. And most earnestly do I beseech Thee to write the truth ever deeper in my heart, as one of the laws of Thy Kingdom, that Loving Obedience may look for a Loving Acceptance, sealed by ever-increasing experience of the Power of the Spirit.

I thank Thee for what Thy word teaches of what the Love and Obedience of Thy disciples were. Though still imperfect--for did they not all forsake Thee?--

yet Thou didst cover it with the cloak of Thy love: 'The spirit is willing, but the flesh weak;' and accept it, feeble though it was. Savior! with my whole heart I say I do love Thee, and would keep each one of Thy commandments.

Afresh I surrender myself to Thee for this. In the depths of my soul Thou seest there is but one desire, that Thy will should be done in me as in Heaven.

To every reproof of conscience I would bow very low. To every moving of Thy Spirit I would yield in implicit obedience. Into Thy death I give my will and life, that, being raised with Thee, the Life of Another even of Thy Holy Spirit, who dwelleth in me, and revealeth Thee, may be my life. Amen.

Chapter 8
Knowing The Spirit.

The Spirit of Truth whom the world cannot receive, for it beholdeth Him not, neither knoweth Him: Ye know Him; for He abideth with you, and shall be in you.' John 14: 17.

'Know ye not that ye are a temple of God, and that the Spirit of God dwelleth in you?' 1 Corinthians 3:16.

The value of knowledge, that is, true spiritual knowledge, in the life of faith can hardly be exaggerated. Just as a man on earth is none the richer for an inheritance that comes to him, or a treasure in his field, as long as he does not know of it, or does not know how to get possessed of it, and to use it,-so the gifts of God's Grace cannot bring their full blessing until we know and, in knowing, truly apprehend and possess them. In Christ are hid all the treasures of wisdom and knowledge; it is the excellency of the knowledge of Christ Jesus, his Lord, for which the believer is willing to count all things but loss. It is owing to the want of a true knowledge of what God in Christ has prepared for us that the lives of believers are so low and feeble. The prayer Paul offered for the Ephesians-- that the Father would give them the Spirit of wisdom and revelation in the knowledge of Him, the eyes of their heart being enlightened, that they might know the hope of their calling, and the riches of the inheritance, and the exceeding goodness of the power working in them-- is one we never can pray enough, whether for ourselves or for others. But of what special importance it is that we should know the Teacher through whom all the other knowledge is to come! The Father has given each one of His children not only Christ, who is the truth, the reality of all life and grace, but the Holy Spirit, who is the very Spirit of Christ and the Truth. ' We received the Spirit, which is of God, that we might know the things which are freely given us by God.'

But now comes the important question, How do we know when it is the Spirit that is teaching us? If our knowledge of Divine things is to be to us a certainty and a comfort, we must know the Teacher Himself. It is only knowing Him that will be to us the full evidence that what we count our spiritual knowledge is no deception. Our blessed Lord meets this question, with all the solemn issues depending upon it, by assuring us that we shall know the Spirit. When a messenger comes to tell of a king, when a witness gives a testimony for his friend, neither speaks of himself. And yet, without doing so, both the messenger and the witness, in the very fact of giving their evidence, draw our attention to themselves, and claim our recognition of their presence and trustworthiness. And just so the Holy Spirit, when He testifies of Christ and glorifies Him, must be known and acknowledged in His Divine commission and presence. It is only thus that we can have the assurance that the knowledge we receive is indeed of God, and not what our human reason has gathered from the Word of God. To know the King's seal is the only safeguard against a counterfeit image. To know the Spirit is the Divine foundation of certainty.

And how now can the Spirit thus be known ? Jesus says: 'Ye know Him, for He abideth with you, and shall be in you.' The abiding indwelling of the Spirit is the condition of knowing Him. His presence will be self-evidencing. As we allow Him to dwell in us, as we give Him full possession in faith and obedience, and allow Him to testify of Jesus as Lord, He will bring His credentials: He will prove Himself to be the Spirit of God. 'It is the Spirit beareth witness, because the Spirit is truth.' It is because the presence of the Spirit as the indwelling teacher of every believer is so little known and recognized in the Church, and because, as the result of this, the workings of the Spirit are few and feeble, that there is so much difficulty and doubt, so much fear and hesitation about the recognition of the witness of the Spirit. As the truth and experience of the indwelling of the Spirit is restored among God's people, and the Spirit is free again to work in power among us, His blessed presence will be its own sufficient proof : we shall indeed know Him. Ye know Him, for He shall be in you."

But meanwhile, as long as His presence is so little recognized, and His working straitened, how is He now to be known ? To this question the answer is very simple. To every one who honestly desires, not only to know that he has the Spirit, but to know Him in His person, and as a personal possession and Teacher, we say: Study the teaching of the Word in regard to the Spirit. Be not content with the teaching of the Church or of men about the Spirit, but go to the Word. Be not content with your ordinary 'reading of the Word, or what you already know of its doctrines. If you are in earnest to know the Spirit, go and search the Word specially with this view, as one thirsting to drink deeply of the water of life. Gather together all the Word says of the Spirit, His indwelling and His work, and hide it in your heart. Be determined to accept of nothing but what the Word teaches, but also to accept heartily of all it teaches.

But study the Word in dependence on the Spirit's teaching. If you study it with your human wisdom, your study of it may only confirm you in your mistaken views. If you are a child of God, you have the Holy Spirit to teach you, even though you do not yet know how He works in you. Ask the Father to work through Him in you, and to make the Word life and light in you. If, in the spirit of humility, and trusting in God's guidance, you submit heartily to the Word, You will find the promise surely fulfilled: you will be taught of God. We have more than once spoken of the progress from the outward to the inward: be whole-hearted in giving up all your thoughts and men's thoughts as you accept the Word; ask God to reveal in you by His Spirit His thoughts concerning His Spirit: He will assuredly do so.

And what will be the chief marks to be found in the Word by which the Spirit in us can be known? They will be chiefly two. The first will be more external, referring to the work He does. The second more in the inner life, in the dispositions which He seeks in those in whom He dwells.

We have just heard how Jesus spoke of a loving obedience as the condition of the Spirit's coming. Obedience is the abiding mark of His presence. Jesus gave Him as a Teacher and Guide. All Scripture speaks of His work as demanding the surrender of the whole life. 'If by the Spirit ye mortify the deeds of the body, ye shall live; for as many as are led by the Spirit of God, these are the sons of God.' ' Your body is a temple of the Holy Ghost: glorify God therefore in your body.' ' If we live in the Spirit, let us also walk in the Spirit.' 'We are changed into the same image, even as by the Spirit of the Lord.' Words like these define very distinctly the operations of the Spirit. As God is first known in His works, so with the Spirit. He reveals God's will, Christ doing that will, - and calling us to follow Him in it. As the believer surrenders himself to a life in the Spirit, cordially consents that the leading of the Spirit, the mortifying of the flesh, the obedience to the rule of Christ, without limit or exception, shall be what he gives himself up to, and as he waits on the Spirit to work all this, he will find and know the Spirit working in him. It is as we simply make the aim of the Holy Spirit our aim, and give up ourselves entirely to what He is to come and work, that we are prepared to know Him as dwelling in us. As we are led by Him to obey God even as Christ did, it will be the Spirit Himself, bearing witness with our spirit, that He dwells in us.

We shall also know Him, and that still more certainly and intimately, as we not only yield ourselves to that life He works, but as we study the personal relation in which a believer stands to Him, and the way in which His working may most fully be experienced. The habit of soul the Spirit desires is contained in the one word-faith. Faith has ever to do with the Invisible, with what appears to man most unlikely. When the Divine appeared in Jesus, in what a lowly form was it hidden ! Thirty years, He lived in Nazareth, and they had seen nothing in

Him but the son of a carpenter. It was only with His baptism that His Divine Sonship came into complete and perfect consciousness. Even to His disciples His Divine glory was often hidden. How much more when the Life of God enters the depths of our sinful being, will it be matter of faith to recognize it! Let us meet the Spirit in holy, humble faith. Let us not be content just to know that the Spirit is in us: that will profit us but little. Let us cultivate the habit, in each -religious exercise, of bowing reverently in silence before God, to give the Spirit, the recognition that is His due, and keep down the will of the flesh that is so ready with its service of God. Let us wait on the Spirit in deep dependence. Let us have a season of quiet meditation, in which we enter the inner temple of our heart, to see that all there is indeed surrendered to the Spirit, and then bow before the Father to ask and expect from Him the mighty working of the Holy Spirit. However little we see or feel, let us believe. The Divine is always first known by believing. As we continue believing, we shall be prepared to know and to see.

There is no way of knowing a fruit but by tasting it There is no way of knowing the light but by being in it and using it. There is no way of knowing a person but by intercourse with him. There is no way of knowing the Holy Spirit but by possessing Him, and being possessed of Him. To live in the Spirit is the only way to know the Spirit. To have Him in us, doing His work, giving us His fellowship, and guiding our whole life, this is the path the Master opens when He says: ' Ye know Him, for He shall be in you.'

Believer! for the excellency of the knowledge of Christ Jesus Paul counted all things but loss. Shall we not do so too ? Shall we not, to know the glorified Christ through the Spirit, give up everything? Oh, let us think of it! the Father hath sent the Spirit that we might fully share in the glory of the glorified Christ! Shall we not give ourselves up to have Him in us, to let Him have all in us, that we may fully know Him, through whom alone we can know the Son and the Father ? Let us even now yield ourselves to the full to the indwelling and teaching of the Blessed Spirit whom the Son hath given us from the Father.

Blessed Father! who hast, in the name of Christ, sent us Thy Holy Spirit, graciously hear my prayer, and grant that I may know Him indeed by having Him within me. May His witness to Jesus be divinely clear and mighty, may His leading and sanctifying be in such holy power, may His indwelling in my spirit be in such Truth and Life, that the consciousness of Him as my Life may be as simple and sure as of my natural life, As the light is the sufficient witness to the sun, may His light be its own witness to the, presence of Jesus.

And lead me, O my Father, in knowing Him to know aright the mystery of Thy Love in giving Him within. May I understand how it was not enough to

Thee to work in me by Thy secret, unknown, Almighty Power, nor even to work through Him who came to the earth to reveal Thee. Thy Son had something more, and better still, for us the Spirit, the Blessed Third in the Godhead, was sent, that Thy Personal Presence, the most intimate union and unbroken fellowship with Thee, might be my portion. The Holy Spirit, Thy very Life and Self, has come to be now the life of my very self, and so take me wholly for Thine own.

O my God, do teach me and all Thy people to know Thy Spirit. Not only to know that He is in us, not only to know somewhat of His working, but to know Him as in His very person He reveals and glorifies the Son, and in Him Thee the Father, Amen.

Chapter 9
The Spirit of Truth

'But when the Comforter is come, whom I will send unto you from the Father, even the Spirit of Truth, which proceedeth from the Father, He shall bear witness of me.' John 15:26.

'When He, the Spirit of Truth, is come, He shall guide you into all the Truth; for He shall not speak from Himself; but whatsoever things He shall hear, these shall He speak.' John 16:13.

God created man in His image; to become like Himself, capable of holding fellowship with Him in His glory. In Paradise two ways were set before man for attaining to this likeness to God. These were typified by the two trees-that of life, and that of knowledge. God's way was the former, ---through life would come the knowledge and likeness of God; in abiding in God's will, and partaking of God's life, man would be perfected. In recommending the other, Satan assured man that knowledge was the one thing to be desired to make us like God. And when man chose the light of knowledge above the life in obedience, he entered upon the terrible path that leads to death.' The desire to know became his greatest temptation; his whole nature was corrupted, and knowledge was to him more than obedience and more than life.

Under the power of this deceit, that promises happiness in knowledge, the human race is still led astray. And nowhere does it show its power more terribly than in connection with the true religion and God's own revelation of Himself. Even where the word of God is accepted, the wisdom of the world and of the flesh ever enters in; even spiritual Truth is robbed of its power when held, not in the life of the Spirit, but in the wisdom of man. Where Truth enters into the inward parts, as God desires, there it becomes the life of the Spirit. But it may also only reach the outer parts of the soul, the intellect and reason, and while it occupies and pleases there, and satisfies us with the imagination that it will thence exercise its influence, its power is nothing more than that of human argument and wisdom, that never reaches to the true life of the spirit. For there is a truth of the understanding and feelings, which is Only natural, the human image or form, the shadow of Divine Truth. There is a Truth which is substance and reality, communicating to him who holds it the actual possession, the life of the things of which others only think and speak. The truth in shadow, in form, in thought,was all the law could give; and in that the religion of the Jews consisted. The truth of substance, the Truth as a Divine life, was what Jesus brought as the Only-begotten, full of grace and truth. He is Himself 'the Truth.'

In promising the Holy Spirit to His disciples, our Lord speaks of Him as the Spirit of Truth. That Truth, which He Himself is, that Truth and Grace and Life which He brought from heaven as a substantial spiritual reality to communicate to us, that Truth has its existence in the Spirit of God: He is the Spirit, the inner life of that Divine Truth. And when we receive Him, and just as far as we receive Him, and give up to Him, He makes Christ, and the Life of God, to be Truth in us divinely real; He gives it to be in us of a truth. In His teaching and guiding into the Truth, He does not give us only words and thoughts and images and impressions, coming to us from without, from a book or a teacher outside of us. He enters the secret roots of our life, and plants the Truth of God there as a seed, and dwells in it as a Divine Life. And where, in faith, and expectation, and surrender, this Hidden Life is cherished and nourished, there He quickens and strengthens it, so that it grows stronger and spreads its branches through the whole being. And so, not from without but from within, not in word but in power, in Life and Truth, the Spirit reveals Christ and all He has for us. He makes the Christ, who has been to us so much only an image, a thought, a Savior outside and above us, to be Truth within us. The Spirit brings with His incoming the Truth into us ; and then, having possessed us from within, guides us, as we can bear it, into all the truth.

In His promise to send the Spirit of Truth from the Father, our Lord very definitely tells us what His principal work would be-- 'He shall bear witness of ME.' He had just before said,'I am the Truth;' the Spirit of Truth can have no work but just to reveal and impart the fullness of Grace and Truth that there are in Christ Jesus. He came down from the glorified Lord in heaven to bear witness--within us, and so through us, of the reality and the power of the redemption which Christ has accomplished there. There are Christians who are afraid that to think much of the Spirit's presence within us will lead us away from the Savior above us. A looking within to ourselves may do this; we may be sure that the silent, believing, adoring recognition of the Spirit within us will only lead to a fuller, a more true and spiritual apprehension that Christ alone is indeed all in all. 'He shall bear witness of me.' ' He shall glorify me.' It is He will make our knowledge of Christ Life and Truth, and experience of the Power with which He works and saves.'

To know what the disposition or state of mind is in which we can fully receive this guiding into all Truth, note the remarkable words our Lord uses concerning the Spirit: ' He shall guide you into all the Truth, for He shall not speak from Himself; but whatsoever things He shall hear, these shall He speak.' The mark of this Spirit of Truth is a wondrous Divine Teachableness. In the mystery of the Holy Trinity there is nothing more beautiful than this, that with a Divine equality on the part of the Son and the Spirit, there is also a perfect subordination. The Son could claim that men should honor Him even as they honored the Father, and yet counted it no derogation from that honor to say, The Son can do nothing of Himself; as I hear, so I speak. And even so the Spirit of Truth never speaks from Himself. We should think He surely could speak from Himself; but no, only what He hears, that He speaks. The Spirit that fears to speak out of its own, that listens for God to speak, and only speaks when God speaks, this is the Spirit of Truth.

And this is the disposition He works, the life He breathes, in those who truly receive Him---that gentle teachableness which marks the poor in spirit, the broken in heart, who have become conscious that as worthless as their righteousness, is their wisdom, or power of apprehending spiritual truth ; that they need Christ as much for the one as the other, and that the Spirit within them alone can be the Spirit of Truth. He shows us how, even with the word of God in our hands and on our tongues, we may be utterly wanting in that waiting, docile, submissive spirit to which alone its spiritual meaning can be revealed. He opens our eyes to the reason why so much Bible reading, and Bible knowledge, and Bible preaching has so little fruit unto true holiness; because it is studied and held with a wisdom that is not from above, that was not asked for and waited for from God. The mark of the Spirit of Truth was wanting. He speaketh not, He thinketh not from Himself ; what He hears, that He speaks. The Spirit of Truth receives everything day by day, step by step, from God in heaven. He is silent, and does not speak, except and until He hears.

These thoughts suggest to us the great danger of the Christian life-seeking to know the Truth of God in His word without the distinct waiting on the Spirit of Truth in the heart. The tempter of Paradise still moves about among men. Knowledge is still his great temptation. How many Christians there are who could confess that their knowledge of Divine Truth does but little for them: it leaves them powerless against the world and sin; they know little of the light and the liberty, the strength and the joy the Truth was meant to bring. It is because they take to themselves God's truth in the power of human wisdom and human thought, and wait not for the Spirit of Truth to lead 'them into it.' Most earnest efforts to abide in Christ, to walk like Christ, have failed because their faith stood more in the wisdom of man than in the power of God. Most blessed experiences have been short lived, because they knew not that the Spirit of Truth was within them to make Christ and His Holy Presence an abiding reality.

These thoughts suggest the great need of the Christian life. Jesus said, 'If any man will come after me, let him deny himself, and follow me.' Many a one follows Jesus without denying himself, And there is nothing that more needs denying than our own wisdom, the energy of the fleshly mind, as it exerts itself in the things of God.

Let us learn that in all our intercourse with God, in His word or prayer, in every act of worship, the first step ought to be a solemn act of abnegation, in which we deny our power to understand God's word, or to speak our words to Him, without the special Divine leading of the Holy Spirit. Christians need to deny even more than their own righteousness, their own wisdom; this is often the most difficult part of the denial of self. In all worship we need to realize the alone sufficiency and the absolute indispensableness, not only of the Blood, but as much of the Spirit of Jesus. This is the meaning of the call to be silent unto God, and in quiet to wait on Him ; to hush the rush of thoughts and words in God's presence, and in deep humility and stillness to wait, and listen, and hear what God will say. The Spirit of Truth never speaks from Himself: what He hears, that He speaks. A lowly, listening, teachable spirit is the mark of the presence of the Spirit of Truth.

And then, when we do wait, let us remember that even then the Spirit of Truth does not at once or first speak in thoughts that we can at once apprehend and express. These are but on the surface. To be true they must be rooted deep. They must have hidden depth in themselves. The Holy Spirit is the Spirit of Truth because He is the Spirit of Life: the Life is the Light. Not to thought or feeling does He speak in the first place, but in the hidden man of the heart, in the spirit of a man which is within him, in his inmost parts. It is only to faith that it is revealed what His teaching means, and what His guidance into the Truth. Let our first work therefore today again be to believe ; that is, to recognize the Living God in the work He undertakes to do. Let us believe in the Holy Spirit as the Divine Quickener and Sanctifier, who is already within us, and yield up all to Him. He will prove Himself the Divine Enlightener: the Life is the Light. Let the confession that we have no life or goodness of our own be accompanied by the confession that we have no wisdom either; the deeper our sense of this, the more precious will the promise of the Spirit's guidance become. And the deep assurance of having the Spirit of Truth within us will work in us the holy teacher's likeness, and the quiet hearkening to which the secrets of the Lord shall be revealed.

O Lord God of Truth! in them that worship Thee, Thou seekest Truth in the inward parts. I do bless Thee again that Thou hast given me too the Spirit of Truth, and that He now dwells in me. I bow before Thee in lowly fear to ask that I may know Him aright, and walk before Thee in the living consciousness that the Spirit of Truth, the Spirit of Christ, who is the Truth, is indeed within me, the inmost self of my new life. May every thought and word, every disposition and habit, be the proof that the Spirit of Christ, who is the Truth, dwells and rules within me.

Especially do I ask Thee that He may witness to me of Christ Jesus. May the Truth of His atonement and blood, as it works with living efficacy in the upper sanctuary, dwell in me and I in it. May His Life and Glory no less be Truth in me, a living experience of His Presence and Power. 0 my Father ! may the Spirit of Thy Son, the Spirit of Truth, indeed be my life. May each word of Thy Son through Him be made true in me.

I do thank Thee once again, O my Father, that He dwelleth within me. I bow my knees that Thou wouldest grant that, according to the riches of Thy glory, He may work mightily in me and all Thy saints. Oh, that all Thy people may know this their privilege and rejoice in it: the Holy Spirit within them to reveal Christ, full of Grace and Truth, as Truth in them. Amen.

Chapter 10
The Expediency of the Spirit's Coming

'I tell you the truth; it is expedient for you that I go away: for if I go not away, the Comforter will not come ; but if I go, I will send Him unto YOU.'
John 16:7.

As our Lord is leaving this world, He promises the disciples here that His departure will be their gain ; the Comforter will take His place, and be to them far better than He ever had been or could be in His bodily presence. This very specially in two aspects. His intercourse with them had never been unbroken, but liable to interruption; now it would even be broken off by death, and they would see Him no more. The Spirit would abide with them for ever. His own intercourse had been very much external, and, in consequence of this, had not resulted in what might have been expected. The Spirit would be in them; His coming would be as an Indwelling Presence, in the power of which they should have Jesus too in them as their Life and their Strength.

During the life of our Lord on earth, each of His disciples was dealt with by Him in accordance with his peculiar character, and the special circumstances in which he might be placed. The intercourse was an intensely personal one: in every thing He proved that He knew His sheep by name. For each there was a thoughtfulness and a wisdom that met just what was required. Would the Spirit supply this need too, and give back that tenderness of personal interest and that special individual dealing which had made the guidance of Jesus so precious ? We cannot doubt it. All that Christ had been to them, the Spirit was to restore in greater power, and in a blessedness that should know no break. They were to be far happier and safer and stronger with Jesus in heaven, than they ever could have been with Him on earth. This, the chief beauty and blessedness of their discipleship of such a Master, that He was so wise and patient to give to each one just what he needed and to make each one feel that he had in Him his best friend, could never be left out. The indwelling of the Spirit was meant to restore Christ's most personal intercourse and guidance, His direct personal friendship.

It is to many a matter of great difficulty to conceive of this or to believe it; much less do they experience it. The thought of Christ walking with men on earth, living and guiding them, is so clear; the thought of a Spirit hiding Himself within us, and speaking, not in distinct thoughts, but only in the secret depths of the life, makes His guidance so much more difficult.

And yet just what constitutes the greater difficulty of the new, the spiritual intercourse and guidance, is what gives it its greater worth and blessedness. It is the same principle we see in daily life: difficulty calls out the powers, strengthens the will, develops character, and makes the man. In a child's first lessons he has to be helped and encouraged ; as he goes on to what is more difficult, the teacher leaves him to his own resources. A youth leaves his parents' roof to have the principles that have been instilled tested and strengthened. In each case it is expedient that the outward presence and help be withdrawn, and the soul be thrown upon itself to apply and assimilate the lessons it had been taught. God wants to educate us, indeed, to a perfect manhood, not ruled by an outward law, but by the inner life. As long as Jesus was with the disciples on earth, He had to work from without inward, and yet could never effectually reach or master the inmost parts. When He went away He sent the Spirit to be in them, that now their growth might be from within outward. Taking possession first by His Spirit of the inmost secret recesses of their being, He would have them, in the voluntary consent and surrender to His inspiration and guidance, personally become what He Himself is, through His Spirit in them. So they would have the framing of their life, the forming of their character, in their own hands, in the power of the Divine Spirit, who really had become their spirit. So they would grow up to that true self-standingness, that true independence of the outward, in which they should become like Himself, a true, separate person, having life in himself, and yet only living in the Father.

As long as the Christian only asks what is easy and pleasant, he will never understand that it is expedient, really better for us, that Christ should not be on earth. But as soon as the thoughts of difficulty and sacrifice are set aside, in the honest desire to become a truly God-like man, bearing the full image of the first-born Son, and in all things living well pleasing to the Father, the thought of Jesus' departure that His Spirit may now become our very own, and we be exercised and disciplined in the life of faith, will be welcomed with gladness and gratitude. If to follow the leading of the Spirit, and experience the personal friendship and guidance of Jesus in it, be a much more difficult and dangerous path than it would have been to follow Him on earth, we must remember the privilege we enjoy, the nobility we attain, the intimacy of fellowship with God we enter into, - all these are infinitely greater. To have the Holy Spirit of God coming through the human nature of our Lord, entering, into our spirits, identifying Himself with us, and becoming our very own just as He was the

Spirit of Christ Jesus on earth, surely this is a blessedness worth any sacrifice, for it is the beginning of the indwelling of God Himself.

But to see that it is such a privilege and to desire it very earnestly does not remove the difficulty. And so the question comes again: the intercourse of Jesus with His disciples on earth, so condescending in its tenderness, so particular and minute in its interest, so consciously personal in its love, how can this be ours in the same degree now that He is absent, and the Spirit is to be our guide ? The first answer here, is, as through the whole Christian life, by faith. With Jesus on earth, the disciples, when once they had believed, walked by sight, We walk by faith. In faith, we must accept and rejoice in the word of Jesus: 'It is expedient for you that I go away.' We must take time distinctly to believe it, to approve of it, to rejoice that He is gone to the Father. We must learn to thank and praise Him that He has called us to this life in the Spirit. We must believe that in this gift of the Spirit the presence and intercourse of our Lord are fully secured to us most certainly and effectually. It may indeed be in a way we do not yet understand, because we have so little believed and rejoiced in the gift of the Holy Spirit. But faith must believe and praise for what it does not yet understand; let us believe assuredly and joyfully that the Holy Spirit, and Jesus Himself through Him, will teach us how the intercourse and guidance are to be enjoyed.

Will teach us. Beware of misunderstanding these words. We always connect teaching with thoughts. We want the Spirit to suggest to us certain conceptions of how Jesus will be with us and in us. And this is not what He does. The Spirit does not dwell in the mind, but in the life. Not in what we know, but in what we are does the Spirit begin His work. Do not let us seek or expect at once a clear apprehension, a new insight, into this or any Divine truth. Knowledge, thought, feeling, action, all this is a part of that external religion which the external presence of Jesus had also wrought in the disciples. The Spirit was now to come, and, deeper down than all these, He was to be the Hidden Presence of Jesus within the depths of their personality. The Divine Life was in a newness of power to become their life. And the teaching of the Spirit would begin, not in word or thought, but in Power. In the Power of a Life working in them secretly, but with Divine energy; in the Power of a Faith that rejoiced that Jesus was really near, was really taking charge of the whole life and every circumstance of it; the Spirit would inspire them with the faith of the Indwelling Jesus. This would be the beginning and the blessedness of His teaching. They would have the Life of Jesus within them, and they would by faith know that it was Jesus: their faith would be at once cause and effect of the Presence of the Lord in the Spirit.

It is by such a faith--a faith which the Spirit breathes, which comes from His being and living in us--that the Presence of Jesus is to be as real and all-sufficient as when He was on earth. But why then is it that believers who have the Spirit do not experience it more consciously and fully! The answer is very simple: they know and honour the Spirit who is in them so little. They have much faith in Jesus who died, or who reigns in heaven, but little faith in Jesus who dwells in them by His Spirit. It is this we need: faith in Jesus as the fulfiller of the promise, 'He that believeth in me, rivers of living water shall flow out of him.' We must believe that the Holy Spirit is within us as the Presence of our Lord Jesus. And we must not only believe this with the faith of the understanding as it seeks to persuade itself of the truth of what Christ says. We must believe with the heart, a heart in which the Holy Spirit dwells. The whole gift of the Spirit, the whole teaching of Jesus concerning the Spirit, is to enforce the word: 'The Kingdom of God is within you.' If we would have the true faith of the heart, let us turn inward, and very gently and humbly yield to the Holy Spirit to do His work in us.

To receive this teaching and this faith, which standeth in the Life and Power of the Spirit, let us above all fear that which hinders Him most, -- will and the wisdom of man. We are still surrounded by a life of self, of the flesh ; in the service of God, even in the effort to exercise faith, it is ever putting itself forward, and putting forth its strength. Every thought, not only every evil thought, but every thought, however good, in which our mind runs before the Spirit, must be brought into captivity. Let us lay our own will and our own wisdom captive at the feet of Jesus, and wait in faith and holy stillness of soul there. The deep, consciousness will grow strong that the Spirit is within us, and that His Divine Life is living and growing within us. As we thus honor Him, and give up to Him, as we bring our fleshly activity into subjection and wait on Him, He will not put us to shame, but do His work within us. He will strengthen our inner life; He will quicken our faith; He will reveal Jesus; and we shall, step by step, learn that the Presence and Personal Intercourse and Guidance of Jesus are ours as clearly and sweetly, yea, more truly and mightily, than if He were with us on earth.'

Blessed Lord Jesus! I do rejoice that Thou art no longer here on earth. I do bless Thee that in a fellowship more real, more near, more tender, more effectual than if Thou wert still here on earth, Thou dost manifest Thyself to Thy disciples. I do bless Thee that Thy Holy Spirit dwells within me, and gives me to know what that fellowship is, and what the realness of Thy holy indwelling.

Most Holy Lord! forgive that I have not known Thy Spirit sooner and better, that I have not praised and loved Thee aright for this most wonderful gift of

Thine and the Father's love. And do teach me in the fullness of faith to believe in Thee, from whom, day by day, the fresh anointing flows and fills the life.

And hear me, Lord, when I cry to Thee on behalf of so many of Thy redeemed ones, who do not yet even see what it is to give up and lose the mixed life after the flesh, to receive in its stead the life that is in the power of the Spirit. With many of Thy saints, I do beseech Thee, oh, grant that the Church may be wakened to know how the one mark of her election, the one secret of her enjoyment of Thy Presence, the one power for fulfilling her calling, is that each believer be led to know that the Spirit dwelleth within him, and that the abiding Presence of his Lord with him as Keeper, and Guide, and Friend is indeed his sure portion. Grant it, Lord, for Thy name's sake. Amen.

Chapter 11
The Spirit Glorifying Christ

It is expedient for you that I go away: for if I go not away, the Comforter will not come ; but if I go, I will send Him unto you. . . . He shall glorify me : for He shall take of mine, and declare it unto you.' John 16: 7, 14,

There is a twofold glorifying of the Son of which Scripture speaks. The one is by the Father, the other by the Spirit: the one takes place in heaven, the other here on earth. By the one He is glorified 'in God Himself;' by the other, 'in us' (John 13: 32, 17:10). Of the former Jesus spake: 'If God be glorified in Him (the Son of Man), God shall also glorify Him in Himself, and shall straightway glorify Him.' And again, in the high-priestly prayer, 'Father, the hour is come; glorify Thy Son.... And now, 0 Father, glorify me with Thyself.' Of the latter He said: 'The Spirit shall glorify me.' 'I am glorified in them.'

To glorify is to manifest the hidden excellence and worth of an object. Jesus, the Son of Man was to be glorified when His human nature was admitted to the full participation of the power and glory in which God dwells. He entered into the perfect spirit - life of the heavenly world, of the Divine Being. And all the angels worshipped Him as the Lamb on the Throne. This heavenly, spiritual glory of Christ the human mind cannot conceive or apprehend in truth. It can only be truly known by being experienced, by being communicated and participated in the inner life. This is the work of the Holy Spirit, as the Spirit of the glorified Christ, He comes down as the Spirit of Glory, and reveals the glory of Christ in us by dwelling and working in us, in the life and the power of that glory in which Christ dwelleth. He makes Christ glorious to us and in us. And so He glorifies Him in us, and through us in them who have eyes to see. The Son seeks not His own glory: the Father glorifies Him in heaven, the Spirit glorifies Him in our hearts.

But before this glorifying of Christ by the Spirit could take place, He must first needs go away from His disciples. They could not have Him in the flesh and in the Spirit too; His bodily presence would hinder the spiritual indwelling. They must part with the Christ they had ere they could receive the indwelling Christ glorified by the Holy Spirit. Christ Himself had to give up the life He had ere He could be glorified in heaven or in us. Even so, in union with Him, we must give up the Christ we have known, the measure of the life we have had in Him, if we are indeed to have Him glorified to us and in us by the Holy Spirit.

I am persuaded that just here is the point at which very many of God's dear children need the teaching' 'It is expedient that I go away.' Like His disciples, they have believed in Jesus; they love and obey Him; they have experienced much of the inexpressible blessedness of knowing and following Him. And yet they feel that the deep rest and joy, the holy light and the Divine power of His abiding Indwelling, as they see it in Holy Scripture, is not yet theirs. Now in secret, and then under the blessed influence of the fellowship of the saints, or the teaching of God's ministers in church or convention, they have been helped and wonderfully blessed. Christ has become very precious. And yet they see something still before them, promises not perfectly fulfilled, wants not fully satisfied. The only reason can be this: they have not yet fully inherited the promise: 'The Comforter shall abide with you, and He shall be in you. He shall glorify me.' The 'expediency of Christ's going away, to come again glorified in the Spirit, they do not fully understand. They have not yet been able to say, 'Even though we have known Christ after the flesh, yet now know we Him so no more!

I knowing Christ after the flesh:' it is this must come to an end, must make way for knowing Him in the power of the Spirit. After the flesh : that means, in the power of the external, of words and thoughts, of efforts and feelings, of influences and aids coming from without, from men and means. The believer who has received the Holy Spirit, but does not know fully what this implies, and so does not give up entirely to His indwelling and leading, still, to a great extent, has confidence in the flesh. Admitting that he can do nothing without the Spirit, he still labors and struggles vainly to believe and live as he knows he should. Confessing most heartily, and at times experiencing most blessedly, that Christ alone is his life and strength, it grieves and almost wearies him to think how often he fails in the maintenance of that attitude of trustful dependence in which Christ can live out His life .in him. He tries to believe all there is to be believed of Christ's nearness and keeping and indwelling, and yet, somehow, there are still breaks and interruptions ; it is as if faith is not what it should be--the substance of the things we had hoped for. The reason must be that the faith itself was still too much the work of the mind, in the power of the flesh, in the wisdom of man. There has indeed been a revelation of Christ the Faithful Keeper, the Abiding Friend, but that revelation has been, in part, taken hold of by the flesh and the fleshly mind. This has made it powerless. Christ, the Christ of glory, the doctrine of the Indwelling Christ, has been received into the mixed life, partly flesh and partly spirit. It is only the Spirit can glorify Christ: we must give up and cast away the old way of knowing and believing and having Christ. We must know Christ no more after the flesh. 'The Spirit shall glorify me.'

But what does it mean that the Spirit glorifies Christ? What is this glory of Christ that He reveals, and how does He do it ? What the glory of Christ is we learn from Scripture. We read in Hebrews, 'We see not yet all things made subject to man. But we see Jesus crowned with glory and honor.' To Him all things have been made subject. So our Lord connects His being glorified, in both the passages we have taken as our text, with all things being given to Him. 'He shall glorify me, for He shall take of mine. All things, whatsoever the Father hath, are mine; therefore, said I, that He taketh of mine, and shall declare it unto you.' 'All things that are mine are Thine, and Thine are mine; and I am glorified in them.' In exalting Him above all rule and power and dominion, the Father hath put all things in subjection under His feet: He gave unto Him the Name which is above every name, that in the Name of Jesus every knee should bow. The Kingdom and the Power and the Glory are ever one: Unto Him that sitteth on the Throne, and to the Lamb in the midst of the Throne, be the Glory and the Dominion for ever. It is as sitting on the Throne of the Divine Glory, with all things put in subjection under His feet (Eph. 1:20-22), that Jesus has been glorified in heaven.'

When the Holy Spirit glorifies Jesus in us, He reveals Him to us in this His glory. He takes of the things of Christ and declares them to us. That is not, He gives us a thought, or image, or vision of that glory, as it is above us in heaven; but He shows it to us as a personal experience and possession - He makes us in our inmost life partake of it. He shows Christ as present in us. All the true, living knowledge we have of Christ is through the Spirit of God. When Christ comes into us as a feeble infant; when He grows and increases and is formed within us; when we learn to trust and follow and serve Him --this is all of the Holy Spirit. All this, however, may consist, even as in the disciples, with much darkness and failure. But when the Holy Spirit does His perfect work, and reveals the Glorified Lord, the Throne of His Glory is set up in the heart, and He rules over every enemy. Every power is brought into subjection, every thought into captivity to the obedience of Christ. Through the whole of the renewed nature ,there rises the song, 'Glory to Him that sitteth on the Throne! Though the confession holds true to the end, 'In me, that is, in my flesh, dwelleth no good thing,' the Holy Presence of Christ as Ruler and Governor so fills the heart and life that His Dominion ruleth over all. Sin has no dominion: the law of the Spirit of the Life in Christ Jesus hath made me free from the law of sin and death.

If this be the glorifying of Christ which the Spirit brings, it is easy to see what the way is that leads to it. The Enthronement of Jesus in His glory can only take place in the heart that has promised implicit and unreserved obedience, that has had the courage to believe that He will take His power and reign, and in that faith expects that every enemy will be kept under His feet. It feels that it needs, it is willing to have, it claims and, accepts, Christ as Lord of All, with everything in the life, great or small, taken possession of and guided by Him, through His Holy Spirit. It is in the loving, obedient disciple the Spirit is promised to dwell ; in him the Spirit glorifies Christ.

This only can take place when the fullness of time has come to the believing soul. The history of the Church, as a whole, repeats itself in each individual. Until the time appointed of the Father, who hath the times and seasons in His own hands, the heir is under guardians and stewards, and differeth nothing from a bond-servant. When the fullness of time is come, and faith is perfected, the Spirit of the Glorified One enters in power, and Christ dwells in the heart. Yea, the history of Christ Himself repeats itself in the soul. In the temple there were two holy places-the one before the veil, the other within the veil, the Most Holy. In His earthly life Christ dwelt and ministered in the Holy Place without the veil: the veil of the flesh kept Him out of the Most Holy. It was only when the veil of the flesh was rent, and he died to sin completely and for ever, that He could enter the Inner Sanctuary of the full glory of the Spirit-life in heaven. And just so the believer who longs to have Jesus glorified within the Spirit, must, however blessed his life has been in the knowledge and service of his Lord, learn that there is something better. In him, too, the veil of the flesh must be rent; he must enter this special part of Christ's work through the new and living way into the Holiest of All. ' He hath suffered in the flesh hath ceased from sin.' As the soul sees how completely Jesus has triumphed over the flesh, and entered with His flesh into the Spirit-Life, how perfect in virtue of that triumph is Power over all in our flesh that could hinder, perfect in the power of the Spirit the Entrance ,the Indwelling of Jesus as Keeper and King be, the veil is taken away, and the life hitherto the holy place is now one in the Most Holy, in the full Presence of the Glory.'

This rending of the veil, this Enthronement of Jesus as the Glorified One in the heart, is not always with the sound of trumpet and shouting. It may be thus at times, and with some, but in other cases it takes place amid the deep awe and trembling of a stillness where not a sound is heard. Zion's King comes, meek and lowly,with the Kingdom to the poor in spirit. Without form or comeliness He enters in, and, when thought and feeling fail, the Holy Spirit glorifies Him to the faith that sees not but believes. The eye of flesh saw Him not on the Throne; to the world it was a mystery; and so, just when all within appears feeble and empty, the Spirit secretly works the Divine assurance, and then the blessed experience, that Christ the Glorified has taken up His abode within. The soul knows, in silent worship and adoration, that Jesus is Master, that His Throne in the heart is established in righteousness; that the promise is now fulfilled, The Spirit shall glorify me.'

Blessed Lord Jesus! I worship Thee in the glory which the Father hath given Thee. And I bless Thee for the promise that that glory shall be revealed in the hearts of Thy disciples, to dwell in them and fill them. This is Thy glory, that all that the Father hath is now Thine: of this Thy glory in its infinite fullness and power Thou hast said the Holy Spirit shall take to show it unto us. Heaven and earth are full of Thy glory: the hearts and lives of Thy beloved may be filled with it too. Lord, let it be so !

Blessed be Thy holy name for all in whom the rich beginning of the fulfillment hath already come ! Lord, let it go on from glory to glory. To this end teach us, we pray Thee, to maintain our separation to Thee unbroken: heart and life shall be Thine alone. To this end teach us to hold fast our confidence without wavering, that the Spirit who is within us will perfect His work. Above all, teach us to yield ourselves in ever increasing dependence and emptiness to wait for the Spirit's teaching and leading. We do desire to have no confidence in the flesh, its wisdom, or its righteousness. We would bow ever lower and deeper before Thee in the holy fear and reverence of the faith that Thy Spirit, the Holy Spirit, the Spirit of Thy glory, is within us to do His Divine work. Blessed Lord! let Him rise in great power, and have dominion within us, that our heart may by Him be fully made the Temple and the Kingdom in which Thou alone art glorified, in which Thy glory filleth all. Amen.

Chapter 12
The Spirit Convincing of Sin.

If I go, I will send the Comforter unto you ; and He, when He is come, will convince the world in respect of sin. John 16:7-8

The close connection between the two statements in these words of our Lord is not always noticed. Before the Holy Spirit was to convince the world of sin, He was first to come into the disciples. He was to make His home, to take His stand in them,, and then from out of them and through them to do His conviction work on the world. He shall bear witness of me, and ye shall also bear witness.' The disciples were to realize that the great work of the Holy Spirit, striving with man, convincing the world of sin, could only be done as He had a firm footing on earth in them. They were to be baptized with the Holy Ghost and with fire, to receive the Power from on high, with the one purpose of being the instruments through whom the Holy Spirit could reach the world. The mighty, sin convicting power of the Spirit to dwell in them and work through them: it was for this our blessed Lord sought to prepare them and us by these words. The lessons they teach are very solemn.

1. The Holy Spirit comes to us, that through us He may reach others. The Spirit is the Spirit of the Holy One, of the redeeming God: when He enters us, He does not change His nature or lose His Divine character. He is still the Spirit of God striving with man, and seeking his deliverance. Wherever He is not hindered by ignorance or selfishness, He looks out from the heart as His temple for the work He has to do on the world around, and makes it willing and bold to do that work; to testify against sin, and for Jesus the Savior from sin, He does this very specially as being the Spirit of the crucified and exalted Christ. For what purpose was it that He received the Spirit without measure ? 'The Spirit of the Lord is upon me, because He anointed me to preach good tidings to the poor. He hath sent me to proclaim release to the captives! It was this same Spirit--after Christ through Him had offered Himself unto God, and through Him as the Spirit of Holiness had been raised from the dead-whom He sent down on His Church, that now the Spirit might have a home in them, as He had had it in Himself. And no otherwise and no less than in Himself would the Divine Spirit in them pursue His Divine work, and as a Light shining in, and revealing, and condemning, and conquering the darkness, as ' the Spirit of burning and the Spirit of judgment,' be to the world the power of a Divine conviction and conversion. Not from heaven direct so much, as the Spirit of God, but as the Holy Spirit dwelling in the Church, would He convince the world. 'I will send Him to you, and when He is come, He will convince the world.' It is in and through us that the Spirit can reach the world.

2. The Spirit can only reach others through us by first bringing ourselves into perfect sympathy with Himself. He enters into us to become so one with us that He becomes as a disposition and a life within us; and His work in us, and through us in others, becomes identical with our work.

The application of this truth to the conviction of sin in the world is one of great solemnity. The words of our Lord are frequently applied to believers in reference to the continued conviction of sin which He will ever have to work within them. In this sense they are, indeed, most true. This first work of the Spirit remains to the end the undertone of all His Comforting and Sanctifying work. It is only as He keeps alive the tender sense of the danger and shame of again sinning, that the soul will be kept in its low place before God,-hiding in Jesus as alone its safety and its strength. As the Holy Ghost reveals and communicates the Holy Life of Christ within, the sure result will be a deeper sense of the sinfulness of sin. But the words mean more. If the Spirit through us, through our testimony, whether by word or walk, is to convince the world, He must first convince us, of its sin. He must give us personally such a sight and sense of the guilt of its unbelief and rejection of our Saviour, such a sight and sense of each of its sins, as being at once the cause, the proof, the fruit of that rejection, that we shall in some measure think and feel in regard to the sin as He does. There will be then that inner fitness in us for the Spirit to work through us, that inner unity between our witness and His witness against sin and for God, which will reach the conscience and carry conviction with a power that is from above.

Alas! how easy it is in the power of the flesh to judge others, in the spirit which sees not the beam in our own eye, or which, if we are indeed free from what we condemn, yet does it with a secret, 'Stand by, I am holier than thou.' We either testify and 'work in a wrong spirit and in our own strength, or have not the courage to work at all. It is because we see the sin and the sinfulness of others, but not in a conviction that comes from the Holy Spirit. When He convinces us of the sin of the world, His work bears two marks. The one is the sacrifice of self, in the jealousy for God and His honor, combined with the deep and tender grief for the guilty. The other is a deep, strong faith in the possibility and power of deliverance. We see each sin in its terrible relation to the whole; we see the whole in the double light of the cross. We see sin unspeakably hateful in its awful guilt against God and its fearful power over the poor soul: we see sin condemned, atoned, put away, and conquered in Jesus. We learn to look on the world as God looks upon it in His holiness: hating its sin with such an infinite hatred, and loving it with such a love, that He gives His Son, and the Son gives His life, to destroy it and set its captives free.

May God give His people a true and deep conviction of the sin of the world in its rejection of Christ, even in the midst of its profession of believing in Him and serving Him, as the fitting preparation for the Spirit's using them in convincing the world of sin.

3. To obtain this conviction of sin, the believer needs not only to pray for it, but to have his whole life under the leading of the Holy Spirit. We cannot too earnestly insist upon it, that the many different gifts of the Spirit all depend upon His personal indwelling and supremacy in the inner life, and the revelation in us of the Christ that gave His life to have sin destroyed. When our Lord spake that word of inexhaustible meaning, ' He shall be in you,' he opened up the secret of all the Spirit's teaching, and sanctifying, and strengthening. The Spirit is the Life of God; He enters in, and becomes our Life; it is as He can sway and inspire the life that He will be able to work in us all He wills. It is desirable and useful to direct the attention of the believer to the different operations of the Spirit, that he may neglect or lose nothing through ignorance. But it is still more needful, with each new insight into what the Spirit can work, to get firmer hold of the truth : Let the life be in the Spirit, and the special blessing will not be withheld. Would you have this deep spiritual conviction of the sin of the world such an affecting sense of its terrible reality and power, its exceeding sinfulness, as will fit you for being the man through whom the Spirit can convince sinners, just yield your whole life and being to the Holy Spirit. Let the thought of this wondrous mystery of the nearness, the Indwelling, of the Holy God in you quiet your mind and heart into lowly fear and worship. Surrender the great enemy that opposes Him-- the flesh, the self-life--day by day to Him to mortify and keep dead. Be content to aim at nothing less than being filled with the Spirit of the Man whose glory it is that He gave Himself to death to take away sin, with the whole being and doing under His control and inspiration. As your life in the Spirit becomes healthy and strong, as your spiritual constitution gets invigorated, your eye will see more clearly, your heart feel more keenly, what the sin around you is. Your thoughts and feelings will be those of the Holy Spirit breathing in you; your deep horror of sin, your deep faith in the redemption from it, your deep love to the souls who are in it, your willingness like your Lord to die if men can be freed from sin, will make you the fit instrument for the Spirit to convince the world of its sin.

4. There is one more lesson. We are seeking in this little book to find the way by which we all can be filled with the Spirit. Here is one condition: He must dwell in us as the world's Convincer of sin, I will send Him unto you, and He will convince the world.' Offer yourself to Him to consider, and feel, and bear the sins of those around you. Let the sins of the world be your concern, as much as your own sin. Do they not dishonor God as much as yours ? Are they not equally provided for in the great redemption ? And does not the Spirit dwelling in you long to convince them too ? Just as the Holy Spirit dwelt in the body and nature of Jesus, and was the source of what He felt, and said, and did, and just as God through Him worked out the will of His holy love; so the Spirit now dwells in believers: they are His abode. The one purpose for which there has been a Christ in the world, for which there is now a Holy Spirit, was that sin may be conquered and made an end of. This is the great object for which the baptism of the Spirit and of fire was given, that in and through believers He might convince of sin, and deliver from it. Put yourself into contact with the world's sin. Meet it in the love and faith of Jesus Christ, as the servant and helper of the needy and the wretched. Give yourself to prove the reality of your faith in Christ by your likeness to Him: so will the Spirit convince the world of its unbelief. Seek the full experience of the indwelling Spirit, not for your own selfish enjoyment, but for this one end, that He can do the Father's work through you as He did through Christ. Live, in unity of love with other believers, to work and pray, that men may be saved out of sin: 'then will the world believe that God hath sent Him.' It is the life of believers in self-sacrificing love that will prove to the world that Christ is a reality, and so convince it of its sin of unbelief.

The comfort and success with which a man lives and carries on his business depends much upon his having a suitable building for it. When the Holy Spirit, in a believer, finds the whole heart free and given up to Him as His home, to fill it with God's thoughts of sin and God's power of redemption, He can through such a one do His work. Be assured that there is no surer way to receive a full measure of the Spirit than to be wholly yielded to Him, to let the very mind of Christ in regard to sin work in us. 'He took away sin by the sacrifice of Himself,' through the Eternal Spirit. What the Spirit was in Him, He seeks to be in us. What was true of Him, must in its measure be true of us.

Christians! would you be filled with the Holy Spirit, seek to have a clear impression of this : the Holy Spirit is in you to convince the world of sin. If you sympathize thoroughly with Him in this, if He sees that He can use you for this, if you make His work in this matter your work too, you may be sure He will dwell in you richly, and work in you mightily. The one object for which Christ came was to put away sin; the one work for which the Holy Ghost comes to men is to persuade them to give up sin. The one object for which the believer lives is to join in the battle against sin ; to seek the will and the honour of his God. Do let us be at one with Christ and His Spirit in their testimony against sin. An exhibition of the life and Spirit of Christ will have its effect : the holiness, and the joy, and the love, and the obedience to Christ will convince the world of its sin of unbelief. The Presence of Christ in us through the Spirit will carry its own conviction. And just as Christ's death, as His sacrifice for sin, was the entrance to His glory in the power of the Spirit, so our experience of the Spirit's indwelling will become the fuller just as our whole life is more given up to Him for His holy work of convincing the world of sin.

Blessed Lord Jesus! it is by the Presence and Power of the Holy Spirit in Thy people that the world is to be convinced of its sin in rejecting Thee, and that sinners are to be brought out of the world to accept of Thee. It is in men and women full of the Holy Ghost, testifying in the power of a holy joy to what Thou hast done for them, that the proof is to be given that Thou art indeed at the right hand of God. It is in a body of living witnesses to what Thou hast done for them, that the world is to find the irresistible conviction of its folly and guilt.

Alas! Lord, how little the world has seen of this. We do call upon Thee, in deep humiliation, Lord Jesus, make haste and rouse Thy Church to the knowledge of its calling. Oh that every believer in his personal life, and all Thy believing people in their fellowship, might prove to the world what reality, what blessedness, what power there is in the faith of Thee ! May the world believe that the Father hath sent Thee, and has loved them as He loveth Thee.

Lord Jesus, lay the burden of the sin of the world so heavy on the hearts of Thy people, that it may become impossible for them to live for anything but this; to be the members of Thy body, in whom Thy Spirit dwells, and to prove Thy presence to the world. Take away everything that hinders Thee from manifesting Thy presence and saving power in us. Lord Jesus, Thy Spirit is come to us to convince the world: let Him come and work in ever-growing power. Amen.

Chapter 13
Waiting for the Spirit.

He charged them to wait for the promise of the Father, which said he, ye heard from me.' Acts 1: 4.

In the life of the Old Testament saints ,waiting was one of the loved words in which they expressed the posture of their souls towards God. They waited for God, and waited upon God. Sometimes we find it in Holy Scripture as the language of an experience: 'Truly my soul waiteth upon God.' 'I wait for the Lord, my soul doth wait.' At others it is a plea in prayer: 'Lead me, on Thee do I wait all the day.' ' Be gracious unto us; we have waited for Thee,' Frequently it is an injunction, encouraging to perseverance in a work that is not without its difficulty: 'Wait on the Lord; wait, I say, on the Lord.' 'Rest in the Lord, and wait patiently for Him.' And then again there is the testimony to the blessedness of the exercise: 'Blessed are they that wait upon Him.' 'They that wait upon the Lord shall renew their strength.'

All this blessed teaching and experience of the saints who have gone before, our Lord gathers up and connects specially, in His use of the word, with the promise of the Father, the Holy Spirit. What had been so deeply woven into the very substance of the religious life and language of God's people was now to receive a new and a higher application. As they had waited for the manifestation of God, either in the light of His countenance on their own souls, or in special interposition for their deliverance, or in His coming to fulfill His promises to His people; so we too have to wait. But now that the Father has been revealed in the Son, and that the Son has perfected the great redemption, now the waiting is specially to be occupied with the fulfillment of the great Promise in which the love of the Father and the grace of the Son are revealed and made ours the Gift, the Indwelling, the fullness of the Holy Spirit. We wait on the Father and the Son for ever-increasing inflowings and workings of the Blessed Spirit; we wait for the Blessed Spirit, His moving, and leading, and mighty strengthening, to reveal the Father and the Son within, and to work in us all the holiness and service to which the Father and the Son are calling us.

'He charged them to wait for the promise of the Father, which ye have heard of me.' It may be asked whether these words have not exclusive reference to the outpouring of the Spirit on the day of Pentecost, and whether, now that the Spirit has been given to the Church, the charge still holds good. It may be objected that, for the believer who has the Holy Spirit within him, waiting for the promise of the Father is hardly consistent with the faith and joy of the consciousness that the Spirit has been received and is dwelling within.

The question and the objection open the way to a lesson of the deepest importance. The Holy Spirit is not given to us as a possession of which we have the charge and mastery, and which we can use at our discretion. No. The Holy Spirit is given -to us to be our Master, and to have charge of us. It is not we who are to use Him; He must use us. He is indeed ours; but ours as God, and our position towards Him is that of deep and entire dependence on One who giveth to every one 'even as He will.' The Father has indeed given us the Spirit; but He is still, and only works as the Spirit of the Father. Our asking for His working, that the Father would grant unto us to be strengthened with might by His Spirit, and our waiting for this, must be as real and definite as if we had to ask for Him for the first time. When God gives His Spirit, He gives His inmost Self. He gives with a Divine giving, that is, in the power of the eternal life, continuous, uninterrupted, and never-ceasing. When Jesus gave to those who believe in Him the promise of an ever-springing fountain of ever-flowing streams, He spake not of a single act of faith that was once for all to make them the independent possessors of the blessing, but of a life of faith that, in never ceasing receptivity, would always and only possess His gifts in living union with Himself. And so this precious word wait,-'He charged them to wait,'-with all its blessed meaning from the experience of the past, is woven into the very web of the new Spirit dispensation. And all that the disciples did and felt during those ten days of waiting, and all that they got as its blessed fruit and reward, becomes to us the path and the pledge of the life of the Spirit in which we can live. The fullness of the Spirit, for such is the Father's Promise, and our waiting, are inseparably and for ever linked together.

And have we not here now an answer to the question why so many believers know so little of the joy and the power of the Holy Spirit ? They never knew to wait for it; they never listened ,carefully to the Master's parting words: 'He charged them to wait for the Promise of the Father, which ye have heard of me'. The Promise they have heard. For its fulfillment they have longed. In earnest prayer they have pleaded for it. They have gone burdened and mourning under the felt want. They have tried to believe, and tried to lay hold, and tried to be filled with the Spirit. But they have never known what it was with it all to wait. They have never here said,or even truly heard, 'Blessed are all they that wait for

Him.' 'They that wait on the Lord shall renew their strength.'

But what is this waiting? And how are we to wait ? I look to God by His Holy Spirit to teach me to state in the simplest way possible what may help some child of His to obey this charge. And let me then first say that, as a believer, what you are to wait for is the fuller manifestation of the Power of the Spirit within you. On the resurrection morn Jesus had breathed on His disciples, and said, Receive the Holy Ghost : they had yet to wait for the full baptism of fire and of power. As God's child you have the Holy Ghost. Study the passages in the Epistles addressed to believers full of failings and sins (1 Cor. 3:1-3, 16, 6:19, 20; Gal. 3:2, 3, 4:6). Begin in simple faith in God's word to cultivate the quiet assurance: The Holy Spirit is dwelling within me. If you are not faithful in the less, you cannot expect the greater. Acknowledge in faith and thanks that the Holy Spirit is in you. Each time you enter your closet to speak to God, sit first still to remember and believe that the Spirit is within you as the Spirit of prayer who cries Father! within you. Appear before God and confess to Him distinctly, until you become fully conscious of it yourself, that you are a temple of the Holy Ghost.

Now you are in the right posture for taking the second step, that is, asking God very simply and quietly, there and then, to grant you the workings of His Holy Spirit. The Spirit is in God and is in you. You ask the Father who is in heaven that His Almighty Spirit may come forth from Him in greater life and power, and as the indwelling Spirit may work more mightily in you. As you ask this on the ground of the promises, or of some special promise you lay before Him, you believe that He hears and that He does it. You have not to look at once whether you feel anything in your heart; all may be dark and cold there; you are to believe, that is, to rest in what God is going to do, yea, is doing, though you feel it not.

And then comes the waiting. Wait on the Lord; wait for the Spirit. In great quietness set your soul still, silent unto God, and give the Holy Spirit time to quicken and deepen in you the assurance that God will grant Him to work mightily. We are a 'holy priesthood to offer up spiritual sacrifice.' The slaying of the sacrifice was an essential part of the service. In each sacrifice you bring there must be the slaying, the surrender and sacrifice of self and its power to the death, As you wait before God in holy silence, He sees in it the confession that you have nothing,-no wisdom to pray aright, no strength to work aright, Waiting is the expression of need, of emptiness. All along through the Christian life these go together , the sense of poverty and weakness, and the joy of all sufficient riches and strength. It is in waiting before God that the soul sinks down into its own nothingness, and is lifted up into the Divine assurance that God has accepted its sacrifice and will fulfill its desires.

When thus the soul, has waited upon God, it has to go forward to the daily walk or the special duty that waits it, in the faith that He will watch over the fulfillment of His Promise and His child's expectation. If it is to prayer you give yourself, after thus waiting for the Spirit, or to the reading of the word, do it in the trust that the Holy Spirit within guides your prayer and your thoughts. If your experience appears to prove that it is not so, be sure this is simply to lead you onwards to a simpler faith and a more entire surrender. You have become so accustomed to the worship in the power of the understanding and the carnal mind, that truly spiritual worship does not come at once. But wait on: 'He charged them to wait.' Keep up the waiting disposition in daily life and duty. 'On Thee do I wait all the day:' it is to the Three One God I thus speak; the Holy Spirit brings nigh and unites to Him. Renew each day and, as you are able to do it, also extend, your exercise of waiting upon God. The multitude of words and the fervency of feelings in prayer have often been more hindrance than help. God's work in you must become deeper, more spiritual, more directly wrought of God Himself. Wait for the promise in all its fullness. Count not the time lost you thus give to this blessed expression of ignorance and emptiness, of faith and expectation, of full and real surrender to the dominion of the Spirit. Pentecost is meant to be for all times the proof of what the exalted Jesus does for His Church from His Throne. The ten days' waiting is meant to be for all time the posture before the Throne, which secures in continuity the Pentecostal blessing, Brother ! the Promise of the Father is sure. It is from whom you have it. The Spirit is Himself already working in you. His full indwelling and guidance is your child's-portion. Oh, keep the charge of your Lord! Wait on God: wait for the Spirit. 'Wait, I say, on the Lord.' 'Blessed are all they that wait for Him.'

Blessed Father ! from Thy Beloved Son we have heard Thy Promise. In a streaming forth that is Divine and never ceasing, the river of the water of life flows from under the Throne of God and the Lamb; Thy Spirit flows down to quicken our thirsty souls. 'For we have not heard, neither hath the eye seen, 0 God, beside Thee, what He hath prepared for him that waiteth for Him.'

And we have beard His charge to wait for the Promise. We thank Thee for what has already been fulfilled to us of it. But our souls long for the full possession, the fullness of the blessing of Christ. Blessed Father! teach us to wait on Thee, daily watching at the posts of Thy doors.

Teach us each day, as we draw near to Thee, to wait for Him. In the sacrifice of our own wisdom and our will, in holy fear of the workings of our own nature, may we learn to lie in the dust before Thee, that Thy Spirit may work with power. Oh, teach us that as the life of self is laid low before Thee day by day, the

Holy Life, that flows from under the Throne, will rise in power, and our worship be in Spirit and in Truth. Amen.

Chapter 14
The Spirit of Power

Ye shall be baptized with the Holy Ghost not many days hence. Ye shall
receive power when the Holy Ghost is come upon you, and ye shall be my
witnesses.' Acts 1: 5, 8.

'Tarry ye in the city, till ye be clothed with power from on high.' Luke 24: 49.

The disciples had heard from John of the Baptism of the Spirit. Jesus had
spoken to them of the Father's giving of the Spirit to those that ask Him, and of
the Spirit of their Father speaking in them. And on the last night he had spoken
of the Spirit dwelling in them, witnessing with them, having come to them to
convince the world. All these thoughts of what this coming of the Holy Spirit
would be were thus connected in their mind with the work they would have to do
and the power for it. When our Lord gathered up all His teaching in the promise,
'Ye shall receive the power of the Holy Ghost coming upon you, and shall be my
witnesses,' it must have been to them the simple summing up of what they
looked for: a new Divine power for the new Divine work of being the witnesses
of a Crucified and Risen Jesus.

This was in perfect harmony with all they had seen in Holy Scripture of the
Spirit's work. In the days before the flood He had been striving with men. In the
ministry of Moses He fitted him, and the seventy who received of his Spirit, for
the work of ruling and guiding Israel, and gave wisdom to those who built God's
house. In the days of the Judges He gave the power to fight and conquer the
enemies. In the times of Kings and Prophets He gave boldness to testify against
sin, and power to proclaim a coming redemption. Every mention of the Spirit in
the Old Testament is connected with the honor and Kingdom of God, and the
fitting for service in it. In the great prophecy of the Messiah, with which the Son
of God opened His ministry at Nazareth, His being anointed with the Spirit had
the one object of bringing deliverance to the captives and gladness to the
mourners. To the mind of the disciples, as students of the Old Testament and
followers of Christ Jesus, the promise of the Spirit could have but one meaning--
fitness for the great work they had to do for their Lord when He ascended the

Throne. All that the Spirit would be to them personally in His work of comforting and teaching, sanctifying the soul and glorifying Jesus, were but as a means to an end--their induement with power for the service of their departed Lord.

Would God that the Church of Christ understood this in our days ! All prayer for the guiding and gladdening influence of the Holy Spirit in the children of God ought to have this as its aim: fitness to witness for Christ and do effective service in conquering the world for Him. Waste of power is always cause of regret to those who witness it. The economy of power is one of the great moving springs in all organization and industry. The Spirit is the great power of God; the Holy Spirit the great power of God's Redemption, as it comes down from the Throne of Him to whom all power has been given. And can we imagine that God would waste this power on those who seek it only for their own sake, with the desire of being beautifully holy, or wise, or good? Truly no. The Holy Spirit is the power from on high for carrying on the work for which Jesus sacrificed His Throne and His Life. The essential condition for receiving that power is that, we be found ready and fit for doing the work the Spirit has come to accomplish.

'My Witnesses:' these two words do indeed contain, in Divine and inexhaustible wealth of meaning, the most perfect description of the Spirit's Work and our work; the work for which nothing less than His Divine power is needed, the work for which our weakness is just fitted. There is nothing so effective as an honest witness. The learned eloquence of an advocate must give way to it. There is nothing so simple: just telling what we have seen and heard, or, perhaps in silence, witnessing to what has been done in us. It was the great work of Jesus Himself: 'To this end have I been born, and to this end am I come into the world, that I should bear witness unto the Truth.' And yet, simple and easy as it appears, to make us witnesses of Jesus is what the Almighty power of the Spirit is needed for, and what He was sent to work. If we are, in the power of the eternal life, the power of the world to come, in heavenly power, to witness of Jesus as He reigns in heaven, we need nothing less than the Divine power of the heavenly life to animate the testimony of our lips and life.

The Holy Spirit makes us witnesses because He Himself is a witness. 'He shall witness of me,' Jesus said. When Peter, on the day of Pentecost, preached that Christ, when He had ascended into heaven, had received from 'the Father the Holy Ghost, and had poured Him forth, he spake of what he knew: the Holy Ghost witnessed to him, and in him, of the glory of his exalted Lord. It was this witness of the Spirit to the reality of Christ's power and presence that made him so bold and strong to speak before the council: 'God did exalt Him to be a Prince and a Saviour; and we are witnesses of these things; and so is the Holy Ghost.' It is as the Holy Spirit becomes to us, in a Divine life and power, the witness to what Jesus is at the present moment in His glory, that our witness will be in His power. We may know all that the Gospels record and all that Scripture further teaches of the person and work of Jesus; we may even speak from past experience of what we once knew of the power of Jesus : this is not the witness of power that is promised here, and that will have effect in the world. It is the Presence of the Spirit at the present moment, witnessing to the Presence of the personal Jesus, that gives our witness that breath of life from heaven that makes it mighty through God to the casting down of strongholds. You can truly witness to just as much of Jesus as the Holy Spirit is witnessing to you in life and truth.

The baptism of power, the induement of power, is sometimes spoken of and sought after as a special gift. If Paul asked very distinctly for the Ephesians who had been sealed with the Holy Spirit, that the Father would still give them 'the Spirit of wisdom' (Eph. 1:17), we cannot be far wrong in praying as definitely for 'the Spirit of power.' He who searches the hearts knows what is the mind of the Spirit, and will give not according to the correctness of our words, but the Spirit-breathed desire of our hearts. Or let us take that other prayer of Paul (Eph.3:16), and plead that ' He would grant us to be mightily strengthened by His Spirit.' However we formulate our prayer, one thing is certain: it is in unceasing prayer, it is in bowing our knees, it is in waiting on God, that from Himself will come what we ask, be it the Spirit of Power or the Power of the Spirit. The Spirit is never anything separate from God; in all His going out and working He still ever is the inmost self of God; it is God Himself who, according to the riches of His glory, is mighty to do above what we ask or think who will in Christ give us to be clothed with the power of the Spirit.

In seeking for this Power of the Spirit, let us note the mode of His working. There is one mistake we must specially beware of. It is that of expecting always to feel the power when it works. Scripture links power and weakness in a wonderful way, not as succeeding each other, but as existing together. 'I was with you in weakness ;my preaching was in power.' 'When I am weak, then am I strong.' (See 1 Cor.2:3-5 ; 2 Cor.4:7,16, 6:10, 7:10, 13:3, 4.) The power is the power of God, given to faith; and faith grows strong in the dark. The Holy Spirit hides Himself in the weak things that God hath chosen, that flesh may not glory in His presence. Spiritual power can only be known by the Spirit of faith. The more distinctly we feel and confess our weakness and believe in the power dwelling within us, ready to work as need arises, the more confidently may we expect its Divine operation even when nothing is felt. Christians lose much not only by not waiting for the power, but by waiting in the wrong way. Seek to combine the faithful and ready obedience to every call of duty, however little thy power appears to be, with a deep, dependent waiting and expectation of Power from on high. 'Let thy intervals of repose and communion be the exercise of prayer and faith in the Power of God dwelling in thee, and waiting to work through thee; thy time exertion and effort will bring the 'proof that by faith out of weakness we are made strong.

Let us also see and make no mistake about the condition of the working of this Divine Power. He that would command nature must first, and most absolutely obey her. It does not need much grace to long and ask for power, even the power of the Spirit. Who would not be glad to have power? Man pray earnestly for power in or with their work, and receive it not, because they do not accept the only posture in which the Power can work. We want to get possession of the Power and use it. God wants the Power to get possession of us, and use us. If we give up ourselves to the Power to rule in us, the Power will give itself to us, to rule through us. Unconditional submission and obedience to the Power in our inner life is the one condition of our being clothed with it. God gives the Spirit to the obedient. 'Power belongeth unto God' and remains His for ever. If thou wouldst have His power work in thee, bow very low in reverence before the Holy Presence that dwelleth in thee, that asks thy surrender to His guidance even in the least things. Walk very humbly in holy fear, lest in anything thou shouldest fail in knowing or doing His holy will. Live as one given up to a Power that has the entire mastery over thee, that has complete possession of thy inmost being. Let the Spirit and His Power have possession of thee: thou shalt know that His power worketh in thee.

Let us be clear, too, as to the object of this power, the work it is to do. Men are very careful to economize power, and to gather it there where it can do its work most effectually. God does not give this power for our own enjoyment,--as little to save us from trouble and effort. He gives it for one purpose, to glorify His Son. Those who in their weakness are faithful to this one object, who in obedience and testimony prove to God that they are ready at any cost to glorify God,-they will receive the power from on high. God seeks for men and women whom He can thus clothe with power. The Church is looking round for them on every side, wondering at the feebleness of so much of its ministry and worship. The world waits for it, to be convinced that God is indeed in the midst of His people. The perishing millions are crying for deliverance, and the Power of God is waiting to work it. Let us not be content with the prayer for God to visit and to bless them, or with the effort to do the best we can for them. Let us give up ourselves, each individual believer, wholly and undividedly, to live as witnesses for Jesus. Let us plead with God to show His people what it means that they are Christ's representatives just as He was the Father's. Let us live in the faith that the Spirit of power is within us, and that the Father will, as we wait on Him, fill us with the power of the Spirit.

Most Blessed Father! we thank Thee for the wonderful provision Thou hast made for Thy children,-that out of weakness they should be made strong, and that just in their feebleness Thy Might Power should be glorified . We thank Thee for the Holy Spirit, as the Spirit of Power, coming down to make Jesus, to whom all Power is given, present with His Church, and to make His disciples the witnesses of that Presence.

I ask Thee, O my Father, to teach me that I have the power, as I have the Living Jesus. May I not look for it to come with observation. May I consent that it shall ever be a Divine strength in human weakness, so that the glory may be Thine alone. May I learn to receive it in a faith that allows the Mighty Lord Jesus to hold the power and do the work in the midst of weakness. And may, by the Holy Spirit, He be so present with me, that my witness may be of Him alone.

O my Father! I desire to submit my whole being to this Holy Power. I would bow before its rule every day and all the day. I would be its servant, and humble myself to do its meanest command. Father I let the Power rule in me, that I may be made meet for it to use. And may my one object in life be that Thy Blessed Son may receive the honour and the glory. Amen.

Chapter 15
The Outpouring of the Spirit.

And when the day of Pentecost was fully come, they were all filled with the
Holy Ghost, and began to speak, as the Spirit gave them utterance.' Acts 1:1-4.

In the outpouring of the Holy Spirit, the work of Christ culminates. The
adorable mystery of the Incarnation in Bethlehem, the great Redemption
accomplished on Calvary, the revelation of Christ as the Son of God in the
power of the Eternal Life by the Resurrection, His entrance into glory in the
Ascension--these are all preliminary stages; their goal and their crown was the
coming down of the Holy Spirit. As Pentecost is the last, it is the greatest of the
Christian feasts ; in it the others find their realization and their fulfillment. It is
because the Church has hardly acknowledged this, and has not seen that the
glory of Pentecost is the highest glory of the Father and the Son, that the Holy
Spirit has not yet been able to reveal and glorify the Son in her as He fain would.
Let us see if we can realize what Pentecost means.

God made man in His own image, and for His likeness, with the distinct
object that he should become like Himself. Man was to be a temple for God to
dwell in ; he was to become the home in which God could rest. The closest and
most intimate union, the indwelling of Love in love : this was what the Holy
One longed for, and looked forward to. What was very feebly set forth in type in
the temple in Israel became a Divine reality in Jesus of Nazareth: God had found
a man in whom He could rest, whose whole being was opened to the rule of His
will and the fellowship of His love. In Him there was a human nature, possessed
by the Divine Spirit; and such God would have had all men to be. And such all
would be, who accepted of this Jesus and His Spirit as their life. His death was
to remove the curse and power of sin, and make it possible for them to receive
His Spirit. His resurrection was the entrance of human nature, free from all the
weakness of the flesh, into the life of Deity, the Divine Spirit-life. His ascension
was admittance as Man into the very glory of God; the participation by human
nature of perfect fellowship with God in glory in the unity of the Spirit. And yet,
with all this, the work was not yet complete. Something, the chief thing, was still
wanting. How could the Father dwell in men even as He had dwelt in Christ ?

This was the great question to which Pentecost gives the answer.

Out of the depths of Godhead, the Holy Spirit is sent forth in a new character and a new power, such as He never had before. In creation and nature He came forth from God as the Spirit of Life. In the creation of man specially He acted as the power in which his god-likeness was grounded, and which, even after his fall, still testified for God. In Israel He appeared as the Spirit of the theocracy, distinctly inspiring and fitting certain men for their work. In Jesus Christ He came as the Spirit of the Father,given to Him without measure, and abiding in Him. All these are manifestations, in different degrees, of one and the same Spirit. But now there comes the last, the long-promised, an entirely new manifestation of the Divine Spirit. The Spirit that has dwelt in Jesus Christ, and, in His life of obedience, has taken up His human spirit into perfect fellowship and unity with Himself, is now the Spirit of the exalted God-man. As the Man Christ Jesus enters the glory of God and the full fellowship of that Spirit-life in which God dwells, He receives from the Father the right to send forth this Spirit into His disciples, yea, in the Spirit to descend Himself, and dwell in them. In a new power, which hitherto had not been possible, because Jesus had not been crucified or glorified, as the very Spirit of the crucified and now glorified Jesus, the Spirit comes. The work of the Son, the longing of the Father, receives its fulfillment. Man's heart is now indeed the home of his God.

Said I not truly that Pentecost is the greatest of the Church's feasts ? The mystery of Bethlehem is indeed incomprehensible and glorious, but when once I believe it, there is nothing that does not appear possible and becoming. That a pure, holy body should be formed for the Son of God by the power of the Holy Spirit, and that in that body the Spirit should dwell, is indeed a miracle of Divine Power. But that the same Spirit should now come and dwell in the bodies of sinful men, that in them too the Father should take up His abode, this is a mystery of grace that passeth all understanding. But this, glory be to God! is the blessing Pentecost brings and secures. The entrance of the Son of God into our flesh in Bethlehem, His entrance into the curse and death of sin as our Surety, His entrance in human nature as First-begotten from the dead into the Power of the Eternal Life, His entrance into the very Glory of the Father--these were but the preparatory steps: here is the consummation for which all the rest was accomplished. The word now begins to be fulfilled: 'Behold! the tabernacle of God is with men, and He shall dwell with them."

It is only in the light of all that preceded Pentecost, of all the mighty sacrifice which God thought not too great if He might dwell with sinful men, that the narrative of the outpouring of the Spirit can be understood. It is the earthly reflection of Christ's exaltation in heaven; the participation He gives to His friends of the glory He now has with the Father. To be apprehended aright, it needs a spiritual vision; in the story that is so simply told the deepest mysteries of the Kingdom are unfolded, and the title-deeds given to the Church of her holy heritage until her Lord's return. What the Spirit is to be to believers and the Church, to the ministers of the word and their work, and to the unbelieving world, are the three chief thoughts.

1. Christ had promised to His disciples that in the Comforter He Himself would again come to them. During his life on earth, His personal manifested Presence, as revealing the unseen Father, was the Father's great gift to men, was the one thing the disciples wished and needed. This was to be their portion now in greater power than before. Christ had entered the glory with this very purpose, that now, in a Divine way, 'He might fill all things,' He might specially fill the members of His body with Himself and His glory-life. When the Holy Spirit came down, He brought as a personal Life within them what had previously only been a Life near them, but yet outside their own. The very Spirit of God's own Son, as He had lived and loved, had obeyed and died, had been raised and glorified by Almighty power, was now to become their personal life. The wondrous transaction that had taken place in heaven in the placing of their Friend and Lord on the throne of heaven, this the Holy Spirit came to be the witness of, yea, to communicate and maintain it within them as a heavenly reality. It is indeed no wonder that, as the Holy Ghost comes down from the Father through the glorified Son, their whole nature is filled to overflowing with the joy and power of heaven, with the presence of Jesus, and their lips overflow with the praise of the wonderful works of God.

Such was the birth of the Church of Christ; such must be its growth and strength. The first and essential element of the true succession of the Pentecostal Church is a membership baptized with the Holy Ghost and with fire, every heart filled with: the experience of the Presence of the glorified Lord, every tongue and life witnessing to the wonderful work God had done, in raising Jesus to the glory of His Throne, and then filling His disciples with that glory too. It is not so much the Baptism of Power for our preachers we must seek; it is that every individual member of Christ's body may know, and possess, and witness to, the Presence of an indwelling Christ through the Holy Spirit. It is this will draw the attention of the world, and compel the confession to the Power of Jesus.

2. It was amid the interest and the questionings which the sight of this joyous praising company of believers awakened in the multitude that Peter stood up to preach. The story of Pentecost teaches us the true position of the ministry and the secret of its power. A church full of the, Holy Ghost is a power of God to awaken the careless, and attract all honest, earnest hearts. It is to such an audience, roused by the testimony of believers, that the preaching will come with power. It is out of such a church of men and women full of the Holy Ghost that Spirit-led preachers will rise up, bold and free, to point to every believer as a living witness to the truth of their preaching and the Power of their Lord.

Peter's preaching is a most remarkable lesson of what all Holy Ghost preaching will be. He preaches Christ from the Scriptures. In contrast with the thoughts of man, who had rejected Christ, He sets forth the thoughts of God, who had sent Christ, who delighted in Him, and had now exalted Him at His right hand. All preaching in the power of the Holy Spirit will be thus. The Spirit is the Spirit of Christ, the Spirit of His personal life, taking possession of our personality, and witnessing with our spirit to what Christ has won for us. The Spirit has come for the very purpose of continuing the work Christ had begun on earth, of making men partakers of His redemption and His life. It could not be otherwise; the Spirit always witnesses to Christ. He did so in the Scriptures; He does so in the believer; the believer's testimony will ever be according to Scripture. The Spirit in Christ, the Spirit in Scripture, the Spirit in the Church; as long as this threefold cord is kept intertwined, it cannot be broken.

3. The effect of this preaching was marvellous, but not more marvellous than might be expected. The Presence and Power of Jesus are such a reality in the company of disciples; the Power from on High, from the Throne, so fills Peter; the sight and experience he has of Christ, as exalted at the right hand of God, is such a spiritual reality; that power goes out from him, and as his preaching reaches its application: 'Know assuredly that God hath made Him both Lord and Christ, this Jesus whom ye crucified,' thousands bow in brokenness of spirit , ready -to acknowledge the Crucified One as their Lord. The Spirit has come to the disciples, and through them convinces the world of unbelief. The penitent inquirers listen to the command to repent and believe, and they, too, receive the gift of the Holy Ghost. The greater works Christ had promised to do through the disciples He has done. In one moment lifelong prejudice, and even bitter hatred, give way to surrender, and love, and adoration; from the glorified Lord power has filled his body, and from its power hath gone forth to conquer and to save.

Pentecost is the glorious sunrise of 'that day,' the first of 'those days' of which the prophets and our Lord had so often spoken, the promise and the pledge of what the history of the Church was meant to be. It is universally admitted that the Church has but ill fulfilled her destiny, that even now, after eighteen centuries, she has not risen to the height of her glorious privilege. Even when she strives to accept her calling, to witness for her Lord unto the ends of the earth, she does it too little in the faith of the Pentecostal Spirit, and the possession of His Mighty Power. Instead of regarding Pentecost as sunrise, she too often speaks and acts as if it had been noonday, from which the light must needs begin to wane. Let the Church return to Pentecost, and Pentecost will return to her. The Spirit of God cannot take possession of believers beyond their capacity of receiving Him. The promise is waiting; the Spirit is now in all His fullness. Our capacity of reception needs enlargement. It is at the footstool of the throne, while believers continue with one accord in praise and love and prayer, while delay only intensifies the spirit of waiting and expectation, while faith holds fast the promise, and gazes up on the exalted

Lord, in the confidence that He will make Himself known in power in the midst of His people,--it is at the footstool of the throne that Pentecost comes. Jesus Christ is still Lord of all, crowned with power and glory. His longing to reveal His presence in His disciples, and to make them share the glory life in which He dwells, is as fresh and full as when He first ascended the throne. Let us take our place at the footstool. Let us yield ourselves in strong, expectant faith, to be filled with the Holy Ghost, and to testify for Jesus. Let the indwelling Christ be our life, and our strength, and our testimony. Out of such a Church Spirit-filled preachers will rise, and the power go forth that will make Christ's enemies bow at His feet.

O Lord God! we worship before the Throne on which the Son is seated with Thee, crowned with glory and honor. We thank and bless Thee that it is for us, the children of men, that Thou hast done this, and that He in whom Thou delightest belongs as much to earth as to heaven, to us as to Thee. O God! we adore Thy love: we praise Thy Holy Name.

We beseech Thee, O our Father, to reveal to Thy Church how our Blessed Head counts us as His own body, sharing with Him in His life, His power, and His glory, and how the Holy Spirit, is the bearer of that life and power and glory, is waiting to reveal it within us. Oh, that Thy people might awake to know what the Holy Spirit means, as the real Presence within them of the glorified Lord, and as the clothing with Power from on high for their work on earth. Oh that all Thy people might learn to gaze on their exalted King until their whole being were opened up for His reception, and His Spirit fill them to their, utmost capacity!

Our Father, we plead with Thee, in the name of Jesus, revive Thy Church. Make every believer to be indeed a temple full of the Holy Ghost: Make every church, in its believing members, a consecrated company ever testifying of a present Christ, ever waiting for the fullness of the power from on high. Make every preacher of the word a minister of the Spirit. And let throughout the earth Pentecost be the sign that Jesus reigns, that His redeemed are His body, that His Spirit works, and that every knee shall bow to Him. Amen.

Chapter 16
The Holy Spirit and Missions

Now there were at Antioch, in the church that was there, prophets and teachers, And as they ministered to the Lord and fasted, the Holy Ghost said, Separate me Barnabas and Saul for the work whereunto I have called them. Then, when they had fasted and prayed, and laid their hands on them, they sent them away. So they, being sent forth by the Holy Ghost, went down to Seleucia.' Acts 13: 1-4.

It has been rightly said that the Acts of the Apostles might well have borne the name, The Acts of the Exalted Lord, or, The Acts of the Holy Spirit. Christ's parting promise, 'Ye shall receive power when the Holy Ghost is come upon you; and ye shall be my witnesses, both in Jerusalem and in all Judea and Samaria, and unto the uttermost parts of the earth,' was indeed one of those Divine seed - words in which is contained the Kingdom of heaven in the power of an infinite growth, with the law of its manifestation, and the prophecy of its final perfection. In the Book of the Acts we have the way traced in which the promise received its incipient fulfillment, on its way from Jerusalem to Rome. It gives us the Divine record of the coming and dwelling and working of the Holy Spirit, as the Power given to Christ's disciples, to witness for Him before Jews and heathens, and of the triumph of the name of Christ in Antioch and Rome as the centers for the conquest of the uttermost parts of the earth. The book reveals, as with a light from heaven, that the one aim and purpose of the descent of the Spirit from our glorified Lord in heaven to His disciples, revealing in them His presence, His guidance, and His Power, is to fit them to be His witnesses even to the uttermost parts of the earth. Missions to the heathen are the one object of the Mission of the Spirit.

In the passage we have as our text we have the first record of the part the Church is definitely called to take in the work of missions. In the preaching of Philip at Samaria, and Peter at Caesarea, - we have the case of individual men exercising their function of ministry among those who were not of the Jews under the leading of the Spirit. In the preaching of the men of Cyprus and Cyrene to the Greeks at Antioch we have the Divine instinct of the Spirit of love and life, leading men to open new paths where the leaders of the Church had not yet thought of coming. But this guidance of the Spirit in separating special men was now to become part of the organization of the Church, and the whole community of believers is to be educated to take its share in the work for which the Spirit specially had come down to earth. If the second of Acts is of importance as giving us the induement of the Church for her Jerusalem or home mission work, the thirteenth is of no less interest as her setting apart for definite foreign mission work. We cannot sufficiently praise God for the deepening interest in missions in our days. If our interest is to be permanent and personal, if it is to be a personal enthusiasm of love and devotion to our Blessed Lord and the lost He came to save, if it is to be fruitful in raising the work of the Church to the true level of Pentecostal Power, we must learn well the lesson of Antioch. Mission work must find its initiative and its power in the distinct and direct acknowledgment of the guidance of the Holy Spirit.

It has often been remarked that true mission work has always been born of a revival of religious life in the Church. The Holy Spirit's quickening work stirs up to new devotion to the Blessed Lord whom He reveals, and to the lost to whom He belongs. It is in such a state of mind that the voice of the Spirit is heard, urging the Lord's redeemed to work for Him. It was thus at Antioch. There were certain prophets and teachers at Antioch, spending part of their time in ministering to the Lord and fasting. With the public service of God in the Church they combined the spirit of separation from the world and of self-sacrifice. Their Lord was in heaven; they felt the need of close and continued intercourse, waiting for His orders; they understood that the Spirit that dwelt in them could not have free and full scope for action except as they maintained direct fellowship with Him as their Master, and entered as much as possible into the fellowship of Christ's crucifixion of the flesh. 'They ministered to the Lord and fasted: such were the men, such was their state of mind and their habit of life, when the Holy Spirit revealed to them that He had chosen two of their number to a special work, and called upon them to be His instruments in separating them, in presence of the whole Church, for that work.

The law of the Kingdom has not been changed. It is still the Holy Ghost who has charge of all mission work. He will still reveal His will, in the appointment of work and selection of men, to those who are waiting on their Lord in service and separation. When once the Holy Spirit in any age has taught men of faith and prayer to undertake His work, it is easy for others to admire and approve what they do, to see the harmony of their conduct with Scripture, and to copy their example. And yet the real power of the Spirit's guiding and working, the real personal love and devotion to Jesus as a Beloved Lord, may be present in but a very small degree. It is because a great deal of interest in the missionary cause is of this nature, that there has to be so much arguing and begging and pleading on lower grounds with its supporters. The command of the Lord is known as recorded in a book; the living voice of the Spirit, who reveals the Lord in Living Presence and Power, is not heard.

'It is not enough that Christians be stirred and urged to take a greater interest in the work, to pray and give more: there is a more urgent need. In the life of the individual the indwelling of the Holy Spirit, and the Presence and Rule of the Lord of Glory which He maintains, must again become the chief mark of the Christian life. In the fellowship of the Church, we must learn to wait more earnestly for the Holy Spirit's guidance in the selection of men and fields of labour, in the wakening of interest and the seeking of support : it is in the mission directly originated in much prayer and waiting on the Spirit that His power can specially be expected.

Let no one fear, when we speak thus, that we shall lead Christians away from the real practical work that must be done. There is much that needs to be done, and cannot be done without diligent labour. Information must be circulated; readers must be found and kept; funds must be raised; prayer-meetings must be kept up; directors must meet, and consult, and decide. All this must be done. But it will be done well, and as a service well-pleasing to the Master, just in the measure in which it is done in the power of the Holy Spirit. Oh that the Church, and every member of it, might learn the lesson! The Spirit has come down from heaven to be the Spirit of Missions, to inspire and empower Christ's disciples to witness for Him to the uttermost parts of the earth.

The origin, the progress, the success of missions are all his. It is He who wakens in the hearts of believers the jealousy for the honour of their Lord, the compassion to the souls of the perishing, the faith in His promise, the willing obedience to His commands, in which the mission takes its rise. It is He who draws together to united effort, who calls forth the suitable men to go out, who opens the door, and prepares the hearts of the heathen to desire or to receive the word. And it is He who at length gives the increase, and, even where Satan's seat is, establishes the cross, and gathers round it the redeemed of the Lord. Missions are the special work of the Holy Spirit. No one may expect to be filled with the Spirit if he is not willing to be used for missions. No one who wishes to work or pray for missions need fear his feebleness or poverty: the Holy Spirit is the power that can fit him to take his divinely appointed place in the work. Let every one who prays for missions, and longs for more of a missionary spirit in the Church, pray first and most that in every believer personally, and in the Church and all its work and worship, the power of the Indwelling Spirit may have full sway.

'Then when they had fasted and prayed, they sent them away. So they, being sent forth by the Holy Ghost, went down to Seleucia.' The sending forth was equally the work of the Church and of the Spirit. This is the normal relation. There are men sent forth by the Holy Spirit alone; amid the opposition or indifference of the Church, the Spirit does His work. There are men sent forth by the Church alone ; it thinks the work ought to be done, and does it, but with little of the fasting and praying that recognizes the need of the Spirit, and refuses to work without Him. Blessed the Church and blessed the mission which the Spirit originates, where He is allowed to guide, and where the blessing is waited for from Himself alone. Ten days' praying and waiting on earth, and the Spirit's descent in fire: this was the birth of the Church at Jerusalem. Ministering and fasting, and then again fasting and praying, and the Spirit sending forth Barnabas and. Saul: this was at Antioch the consecration of the Church to be a Mission Church. In waiting and prayer on earth, and then in the power of the Spirit from the Lord in heaven, is the strength, the joy, the blessing of the Church of Christ and its missions.

May I say to any missionary who reads this in his far-off home, Be of good cheer, brother ,The Holy Spirit who is the Mighty Power of God, ,who is the Presence of Jesus within thee, the Holy Spirit is with thee, is in thee. The work is His depend on Him, yield to Him, wait for Him; the work is His, He will do it. May I say to every Christian, be he director, supporter, contributor, helper in prayer or in any other way,in the great work of hastening the coming of the Kingdom.

Brother! be of good cheer. From that time of waiting before the Throne, and that baptism there received, the first disciples went forth until they reached Antioch. There they paused, and prayed, and fasted, and then passed on over to Rome and the region beyond. Let us from these our brethren learn the secret of power. Let us call on every Christian who would be a mission friend and mission worker to come with us and be filled with the Spirit whose is the work of missions. Let us lift up a clear testimony that the need of the Church and the world is, believers who can testify to an indwelling Christ in the Spirit, and prove it too. Let us gather such together in the antechamber of the King's Presence, the waiting at Jerusalem, the ministering and fasting at Antioch; the Spirit does still come as of old in power, He does still move and send forth; He is still mighty to convince of sin and reveal Jesus, and to make thousands fall at His feet. He waits for us: let us wait on Him, let us welcome Him

O God! Thou didst send Thy Son to be the Savior of the world. Thou didst give Him power over all flesh, that He should give eternal life to as many as

Thou hast given Him. And Thou didst pour out Thy Spirit upon all flesh, commissioning as many as received Him to make known and pass on the wondrous blessing. In the Love and Power in which Thy Spirit was sent forth, He likewise sends forth those who yield- themselves to Him, to be the instruments of His Power in glorifying Thy Son. We bless Thee for this Divine and most glorious salvation.

O our God! we stand amazed, and abased, at the sloth and, neglect of Thy Church in not fulfilling her Divine commission; we are humbled at our slowness of heart to perceive and believe what Thy Son did promise, to obey His will and finish His work. We cry to Thee, our God! visit Thy Church, and let Thy Spirit, the Spirit of the Divine Sending forth, fill all her children.

O my Father! I dedicate myself afresh to Thee, to live and labor, to pray and travail, to sacrifice and suffer for Thy Kingdom. I accept anew in faith the wonderful gift of the Holy Spirit, the very Spirit of Christ, and yield myself to His indwelling. I humbly plead with Thee, give me and all Thy children to be so mightily strengthened by the Holy Spirit that Christ may possess heart and life, and our one desire be that the whole earth may be filled with His glory. Amen.

Chapter 17
The Newness of the Spirit.

But now we have been discharged from the law, having died, to that wherein we were holden; so that we serve in newness of the Spirit, and not in oldness of the letter.' Romans 7:6.

If ye are led by the Spirit, ye are not under the law.' Galatians 5:18

The work of the indwelling Spirit is to glorify Christ and reveal Him within us. Corresponding to Christ's threefold office of Prophet, Priest, and King, we find that the work of the Indwelling Spirit in the believer is set before us in three aspects, as Enlightening, Sanctifying, and Strengthening. 'Of the Enlightening it is that Christ specially speaks in His farewell discourse, when He promises Him as the Spirit of Truth, who will bear witness of Him, will guide into all Truth, will take of Christ's and declare it unto us. In the Epistles to the Romans and Galatians His work as Sanctifying is especially prominent: this was what was needed in Churches just brought out of the depths of heathenism. In the Epistles to the Corinthians, where wisdom was so sought and prized, the two aspects are combined; they are taught that the Spirit can only enlighten as He sanctifies (1 Cor.2 , 3:1-3, 16 ; 2 Cor. 3). In the Acts of the Apostles, as we might expect, His Strengthening for work is in the foreground; as the promised Spirit of Power He fits for a bold and blessed testimony in the midst of persecution and difficulty.

In the Epistle to the Church at Rome, the capital of the world, Paul was called of God to give a full and systematic exposition of His gospel and the scheme of redemption. In this the work of the Holy Spirit must needs have an important place. In giving his text or theme (Rom 1:17), 'The righteous shall live by faith,' he paves the way for what he was to expound, that through Faith both Righteousness and Life would come. In the first part of his argument, to v. 11, he teaches what the Righteousness of faith is. He then proceeds (v. 12-21) to prove how this Righteousness, is rooted in our living connection with the second Adam, and in a justification of Life. In the individual (6:1-13) this Life comes through the believing acceptance of Christ's death to sin and His life to God as ours, and the willing surrender (6:14-23) to be servants of God and of righteousness. Proceeding to show that in Christ we are not only dead to sin, but to the law too as the strength of sin, be comes naturally to the new law which His gospel brings to take the place of the old, the law of the Spirit Of life in Christ Jesus.

We all know how an impression is heightened by the force of contrast. Just as the apostle had contrasted (6:13-23) the service of sin and of righteousness, so he here (7:4) contrasts, to bring out fully what the power and work of the Spirit is, the service in the oldness of the letter, in bondage to the law, with the service in newness of the Spirit, in the liberty and power which Jesus through the Spirit gives. In the following passage, Rom. vii. 14-25, and Rom. 8:1-16, we have the contrast worked out; it is in the light of that contrast alone that the two states can be rightly understood. Each state has its key-word, indicating the character of the life it describes. In Rom. 7 we have the word Law twenty times, and the word Spirit only once. In Rom. 8, on the contrary, we find in its first sixteen verses the word Spirit sixteen times. The contrast is between the Christian life in its two possible states, in the law and in the Spirit. Paul had very boldly said, not only, You are dead to sin and made free from sin that you might become servants to righteousness and to God (Rom.6), but also, 'We were made dead to the law, so that, having died to that wherein we were holden, we serve in newness of spirit, and not in, oldness of the letter.' We have here, then, a double advance, on the teaching of Rom. 6. There it was the death to sin and freedom from it, here it is death to the law and freedom from it. There it was newness of life' (Rom. 5: 4), as an objective reality secured to us in Christ; here it is ' newness of spirit' (Rom.7: 6), as a subjective experience made ours by the indwelling of the Spirit. He that would fully know and enjoy the life in the Spirit must know what life in the law is, and how complete the freedom from it with which he is made free by the Spirit.

In the description Paul gives of the life of a believer, who is still held in bondage of the law, and seeks to fulfill it, there are three expressions in which the characteristic marks of that state are summed up. The first is, the word flesh. ' I am carnal (fleshly), sold under sin. In me, that is, in my flesh, dwelleth no good thing' (14, 18). If we want to understand the word carnal, we must refer to Paul's exposition of it in 1 Cor. 3: 1-3. He uses it there of Christians, who, though regenerate, have not yielded themselves to the Spirit entirely, so as to become spiritual.' They have the Spirit, but allow the flesh to prevail. And so there is a difference between Christians, as they bear their name, carnal or spiritual, from the element that is strongest in them. As long as they have the Spirit, but, owing to whatever cause, do not accept fully His mighty deliverance, and so strive in their own strength, they do not and cannot become spiritual. St.

Paul here describes the regenerate man, as he is in himself. He lives by the Spirit, but, according to Gal.5: 25, does not walk by the Spirit. He has the new spirit within him, according to Ezek.36:26, but he has not intelligently and practically accepted God's own Spirit to dwell and rule within that spirit, as the life of His life. He is still carnal.

The second expression we find in ver. 18 'To will is present with me, but how to do that which is good, is not.' In every possible variety of expression Paul (7: 15-2 1) attempts to make clear the painful state of utter impotence in which the law, the effort to fulfill it, leaves a man : ' The good which I would, I do not; but the evil which I would not, that I practice.', Willing, but not doing such is the service of God in the oldness of the letter, in the life before Pentecost (see Matt. 26: 41). The renewed spirit of the man has accepted and consented to the will of God ; but the secret of power to do, the Spirit of God, as indwelling, is not yet known. In those, on the contrary, who know what the life in the Spirit is, God works both to will and to do ; the Christian testifies, ' I can do all things in Him that strengtheneth me.' But this is only possible through faith and the Holy Spirit. As long as the believer has not consciously been made free from the law with its, 'He that doeth these things shall live through them,' continual failure will attend his efforts to do the will of God. He may even delight in the law of God after the inward man, but the power is wanting.

It is only when he submits to the law of faith, 'He that liveth shall do these things,' because he knows that he has been made free from the law, that he may be joined to another, to the living Jesus, working in him through His Holy Spirit, that he will indeed bring forth fruit unto God (see Rom. 7: 4).

The third expression we must note is in verse 23 'I see a different law in my members, bringing me into captivity under the law of sin which is in my members.' This word, captivity, as that other one, sold under sin, suggests the idea of slaves sold into bondage, without the liberty, or the power to do as they will. They point back to what he had said in the commencement of the chapter, that we have been made free from the law; here is evidently one who does not yet know that liberty. And they point forward to what he is to say in chap. 8: 2: 'The law of the Spirit of life in Christ Jesus hath made me free from the law of sin and death.' The freedom with which we have been made free in Christ, as offered to our faith, cannot be fully accepted or experienced as long as there is ought of a legal spirit. It is only by the Spirit of Christ within us that the full liberation is effected. As in the oldness of the letter, so in the newness of the Spirit, a twofold relation exists: the objective or external, the subjective or personal. There is the law over me, and outside of me, and there is the law of sin in my members, deriving its strength from the objective one Just so, in being made free from the law, there is the objective liberty in Christ offered to -my faith, and there is the subjective personal possession of that liberty, in its fullness and power, to be had alone through the Spirit dwelling and ruling in my members, even as' the law of sin had done. This alone can change the plaint of the captive: 'Oh, wretched man that I am, who shall deliver me from -the bondage of this death?' into the song of the ransomed: 'I thank God through Jesus Christ our Lord,' ' The law of the Spirit made me free.'

And how now have we to regard the two states thus set before us in Rom. 7: 14-23 and via. 1-16? Are they interchangeable, or successive, or simultaneous?

Many have thought that they are a description of the varying experience of the believer's life. As often as, by the grace of God, he is able to do what is good, and to live well -pleasing to God, he experiences the grace of chap. 8, while the consciousness of sin or shortcoming plunges him I again into the wretchedness of chap. 7. Though now the one and then the other experience may be more marked, each day brings the experience of both.

Others have felt that this is is not the life of a believer as God would have it , and as the provision of God's grace has placed it within our reach. And as they saw that a life in the freedom with which, Christ makes free, when the Holy Spirit dwells within us, is within our reach, and as they entered on it, it was to them indeed as if now, for ever they had left the experience of Rom. vii far behind, and they cannot but look upon it as Israel's wilderness life, a life never more to be returned to. And there are many who can testify what light and blessing has come to them as they saw what the blessed transition was from the bondage of the law to the liberty of the Spirit.

And yet, however large the measure of truth in this view, it does not fully satisfy. The believer feels that there is not a day that he gets beyond the words, 'In me, that is, in my flesh, dwelleth no good thing.' Even when kept most joyously in the will of God, and strengthened not only to will but also to do, he knows that it is not he, but the grace of God: 'in me dwelleth no good.' And so the believer comes to see that, not the two experiences, but the two states are simultaneous, and, that even when his experience is most fully that of the law of the Spirit of life in Christ Jesus making him free, he still bears about with him the body of sin and death.' The making free of the Spirit, and the deliverance from the power of sin, and the song of thanks to God is the continuous experience of' the power of the endless life as maintained by the Spirit of Christ. As I am led of the Spirit, I am not under the law. Its spirit of bondage, its weakness through the flesh, and the sense of condemnation and wretchedness it works, are cast out by the liberty of the Spirit.

If there is one lesson the believer needs to learn, who would enjoy the full indwelling of the Spirit, it is the one taught in this passage with such force: that the law, the flesh, that self-effort are all utterly impotent in enabling us to serve God. It is the Spirit within, taking the place of the law without, that leads us into the liberty wherewith Christ hath made us free. 'Where the Spirit of the Lord is, there is liberty.'

Beloved Lord Jesus! I humbly ask Thee to make clear to me the blessed secret of the life of the Spirit. Teach me what it is that we are become dead to the law, so that our service of God is no longer in the oldness of the letter. And what that we are married to Another, even to Thyself, the Risen One, through whom we bring forth fruit unto God, serving in the newness of the Spirit.

Blessed Lord! with deep shame do I confess the sin of my nature, that 'in me, that is, in my flesh, dwelleth no good thing,' that 'I am carnal, sold under sin.' I do bless Thee, that in answer to the cry, 'Who shall deliver me from the body of this death?' Thou hast taught me to answer, 'I thank God through Jesus Christ our Lord.' ' The law of the Spirit of life in Christ Jesus made me free from the law of sin and death.'

Blessed Master ! teach me now to serve Thee in the newness and the liberty, the ever-fresh gladness of the Spirit of life. Teach me to yield myself in large and wholehearted faith to that Holy Spirit, that my life may indeed be in the glorious liberty of the children of God, in the power of an indwelling Savior working in me both to will and to do, even as the Father did work in Him. Amen.

Chapter 18
The Liberty of the Spirit

The law of the Spirit of life in Christ Jesus made me free from the law of sin
and death. If by the Spirit ye make to die the deeds of the body, ye shall live.'
Romans. 8:2:13

In the sixth chapter Paul had spoken (vers. 18, 22) of our having been made
free from sin in Christ Jesus. Our death to sin in Christ had freed us from its
dominion: being made free from sin as a Power, as a Master, when we accepted
Christ in faith, we became servants to righteousness and to God. In the seventh
chapter (vers. 1-6) he had spoken of our being made free from the law.

'The strength of sin is the law:' deliverance from sin and the law go together.
And being made free from the law, we had been united to the living Christ, that,
in union with Him, we might now serve in newness of the Spirit (7:4-6). Paul
had, in these two passages (6 and 7:1-6), presented this being made free from sin
and the law, in its objective reality, as a life prepared in Christ, to be accepted
and maintained by faith, According to the law of a gradual growth in the
Christian life, the believer has, in the power of the Spirit with which he has been
sealed, in faith to enter into this union and to walk in it. As a matter of
experience, almost all believers can testify that, even after they have seen and
accepted this teaching, their life is not what they had hoped it would be. They
have found the descent into the experience of the second half of Rom. 7 most
real and painful. It was because there is, as a rule, no other way for learning the
two great lessons the believer needs. The one is the deep impotence of the
human will, under the law urging it to obedience, ever to work out a Divine
righteousness in man's life; the other, the need of the, conscious and most entire
indwelling of the Holy Spirit as the only sufficient power for the life of a child
of God.

In the first half of Rom. 8 we have the setting forth of this latter truth. In the
Divine exposition of the Christian life in this Epistle, as in its growth in the
believer,'there is a distinct advance from step to step. The eighth chapter, in
introducing the Holy Spirit for the, first time in the unfolding of the life of faith,
as we have it in chaps. 6-8, teaches us that it is only as the Spirit definitely

animates our life and walk, and as He is distinctly known and accepted to do this, that we can fully possess and enjoy the riches of grace that are ours in Christ. Let every one who would know what it is to be dead to sin and alive to God, to be free from sin and a bondslave unto God, to be freed from the law, and married to Him who is raised from the dead, come hither to find the strength he needs, in that Spirit, through whom the union with Christ can be maintained as a Divine experience, and His life be lived within us in Power and in Truth.

In the first half of this eighth chapter the second verse is the center. It reveals the wonderful secret of how our freedom from sin and the law may become a living and abiding experience. A believer may know that he is free, and yet have to mourn that his experience is that of a wretched captive. The freedom is so entirely in Christ Jesus, and the maintenance of the living union with Him is so distinctly and entirely a work of Divine power, that it is only as we see that the Divine Spirit 'dwells within us for this very purpose, and know how to accept and yield to His working it, that we can really stand perfect and complete in the liberty with which Christ hath made us free. The life and the liberty of Rom. 6 and 7:1-6 are only fully ours as we can say, 'The law of the Spirit of the life that is in Christ Jesus made me free from the law of sin and death.' Through the whole Christian life the principle rules: 'According to your faith be it unto you.' As the Holy Spirit, the Spirit of faith, reveals the greatness of God's resurrection power working in us, and as faith in the indwelling Spirit submits to receive that power to the full, all that is true for us in Christ Jesus becomes true in our daily personal experience. It is as we perceive the -difference between this and the previous teaching (Rom. 6-7: 6), as we see what a distinct advance it is upon it, the indispensable completion of the wonderful revelation of our life in Christ there made, that the unique and most glorious place which the Holy Spirit as God holds in the scheme of redemption and the life of faith will open up to us. We learn thus, that, as divinely perfect as is the Life of Liberty in Christ Jesus, is also the power of that Life in the Holy Spirit, enabling us to walk in that Liberty. The living assurance and experience of the Holy Spirit's indwelling will become to us the very first necessary of the new Life, inseparable from the Person and Presence of Jesus Christ our Lord.

'The Law of the Spirit of Life in Christ Jesus made us free from the Law of Sin and Death.' Paul here contrasts the two opposing laws; the one of Sin and Death in the members, the other of the Spirit of Life ruling and quickening even the mortal body. Under the former we have seen the believer sighing as a wretched captive. In the second half of Rom. 6, Paul had addressed him as made free from sin, and by voluntary surrender become a servant to God and to righteousness. He has forsaken the service of sin, and yet it often masters him.

The promise, 'Sin shall not'-shall never for a moment-'have dominion over you,' has not been realized. To will is present but how to perform he knows not. '0 wretched man that I am, who shall deliver me from the body of this death ? is the cry of impotence amid all his efforts to keep the law. 'I thank God, through Christ Jesus our Lord,' is the answer of faith that claims the deliverance in Christ from this power that has held him captive. From the Law, the Dominion of Sin and Death in the members, its actual power in working sin, there is deliverance. That deliverance is a new law, a mightier force, an actual power making free from sin. As real as was the energy of sin working in our members, and more mighty, is the energy of the Spirit dwelling in our bodies. It is the Spirit of the Life that there is in Christ. Out of that Life, when filled as it was in the resurrection and ascension with the mighty energy of God's power (Eph.1:17, 2 1), and admitted on the throne to the omnipotence of God as the Eternal Spirit-out of that Life there descended the Holy Spirit, Himself God. The Law, the Power, the Dominion of the Life in Christ Jesus, made, me free from the Law, the Dominion of Sin and Death in my members, with a freedom as real as was the slavery. From the very first beginnings of the New Life, it was the Spirit who breathed faith in Christ. On our first entering into justification, it was He who shed abroad the love of God in our hearts. It was He who led us to see Christ as our Life as well as our Righteousness. But all this was in most cases still accompanied with much ignorance of His Presence, of the great need and the supply of His Almighty Power. As the believer in Rom.7: (14-23) is brought to the discovery of the deep-rooted legality of the old nature, and its absolute impotence, the truth of the Holy Spirit, and of the Mighty Power with which He does make practically free from the Power of Sin and Death is understood as never before, and our text becomes the utterance of the highest faith and experience combined: 'The Law of the Spirit of Life made me free from the Law of Sin and Death.' As real, and mighty, and spontaneous as was the Law of Sin in the members, is now the Law of the Spirit of Life in those members too.

The believer who would live fully in this liberty of the Life in Christ Jesus will easily understand what the path is in which he will learn to walk, Rom.8 is the goal to which Rom. 6 and 7 lead up. In faith he will first have to study and accept all that is taught in these two earlier chapters of his being in Christ Jesus; dead to sin and alive to God, made free from sin and enslaved to God, free from the law, and married to Christ. 'If ye abide in my word ye shall know the truth, and the truth shall make you free.' Let the word of God, as it teaches you your union with Christ, be the lifesoil in which your faith and life daily roots; abide, dwell in it, and let it abide in you. To meditate, to hold fast, to hide in the heart the word of this gospel, to assimilate it in faith and patience, is the way to rise and reach each higher truth the Scripture teaches. And if the passage through the experience of carnality and captivity, which the attempts to fulfill the law we delight in bring, appears to be anything but progress, let us remember that it is just in the utter despair of self that the entire surrender to the Spirit, to bring and keep us in the liberty with which Christ makes free, is born and strengthened. To cease from all hope in the flesh and the law, is the entrance into the liberty, of the Spirit.

To walk in the path of this New Life it will further be specially needful to remember what is meant by the expression the word so distinctly uses, a 'walk after the Spirit.' The Spirit is to lead, to decide and show the path. This implies surrender, obedience, a waiting to be guided. He is to be the ruling Power, we are in all things to live and act under the Law, the legislation, the Dominion of the Spirit. A holy fear to grieve Him, a tender watchfulness to know His leading, an habitual faith in His hidden but most sure presence, a lowly adoration of Him as God, must be the mark of such a life. The words which Paul uses towards the close of this section are to express our one aim - 'If ye, through the Spirit, make to die the deeds of the body, ye shall live.' The Holy Spirit possessing, inspiring, animating all the powers of our spirit and soul, entering even: into the body, and, in the power of His Divine life, enabling us to make and keep dead the deeds of the body, this is what we may count upon as the fulfillment of the word, 'The law of the Spirit of the Life in Christ Jesus made, me free from the law of Sin and Death.' This is that salvation in sanctification of the Spirit' to which we have been chosen.

'We walk by faith:' this is what we specially need to remember in regard to a ' walk after the Spirit.' The visible manifestation of Christ to us, and His work, are so much more intelligible than the revelation of the Spirit within us, that it is here, above all, in seeking the leading of the Spirit, that faith is called for. The Almighty Power of the Spirit hides Himself away in such a real union with our weakness, with our personality in its abiding sense of weakness, that it needs patient perseverance in believing and obeying to come into the full consciousness of His indwelling, and of His having indeed undertaken to do all our living for us. It needs the direct fresh anointing day by day from the Holy One, in fellowship with Christ, the Anointed, and in persevering waiting on the Father. Here, if ever, the word is needed, 'Only believe! Believe in the Father and His promise! Believe in the Son and His life as thine: 'Our life is hid with Christ in God.' Believe in the Spirit, as the bearer, and communicator, and maintainer of the Life and Presence of Jesus ! Believe in Him as already within thee! Believe in His power and faithfulness to work, in a way that is Divine and beyond thy conception, His work in thee! Believe, ' The Law of the Spirit of Life in Christ Jesus made me free from the Law of Sin and Death.' Bow in deep silence of soul before God, waiting on Him to work mightily in thee by His Spirit. As self is laid low, He will do His blessed and beloved work. He will reveal, will impart, will make and keep divinely present Jesus Christ as the Life of thy spirit.

Ever blessed God and Father! we do praise Thee for the wonderful gift of Thy Holy Spirit, in whom 'Thou with Thy, Son comest to make abode in us. We do bless Thee for that wonderful gift of Eternal Life, which Thy beloved Son brought us, and which we have in Jesus Himself, as His own life given to us. And we thank Thee that the Law of the Spirit of the Life in Christ Jesus now makes us free from the Law of Sin and Death.

Our Father! we humbly pray Thee to reveal to us in full and blessed experience what this perfect Law of Liberty is. Teach us how it is the Law of an inner Life, that in joyful and spontaneous power grows up into its blessed destiny. Teach us that the Law is none other than of the Eternal Life, in its power of continuous and unfading being. Teach us that it is the Law of the Life of Christ Jesus, the living Savior Himself, living and maintaining it in us. Teach us that it is the law of the Spirit of Life in Christ Jesus, the Holy Spirit revealing and glorifying Christ in us as an indwelling Presence. 0 Father ! open our eyes and strengthen our faith, that we may believe that the Law of the Spirit is indeed mightier than the Law of Sin in our members, and makes free from it, so that through the Spirit we make dead the deeds of the body, and indeed live the life of Christ.

O Father! teach this to all Thy children. Amen.

Chapter 19
The Leading of the Spirit

An many as are led by the Spirit of God, these are sons of God.'
Rom.8:14.

By very many Christians the leading of the Spirit is chiefly looked for as a suggestion of thoughts for our guidance. In the decision of doubtful questions of opinion or of duty, in the choice of words from Scripture to use, or the distinct direction to the performance of some Christian work, they would be so glad of some intimation from the Spirit of what the right thing is. They long and ask for it in vain. When at times they think they have it, it does not bring the assurance, or the comfort, or the success, which they think ought to be the seal of what is really from the Spirit. And so the precious truth of the Spirit's leading; instead of being an end of all controversy, and the solution of all difficulty, a source of comfort and of strength, itself becomes a cause of perplexity, and the greatest difficulty of all.

The error comes from not accepting the truth we have had to insist upon more than one the teaching and the leading of the Spirit given in the Life, not in the Mind. The Life is stirred and strengthened; the Life becomes the Light. As the ,conformity to this world spirit is crucified and dies, as we deliberate: and keep down the life of nature and the the flesh, we are renewed in the spirit of our mind and so the mind becomes able to prove and know the good and perfect and acceptable will (Rom.12:2).

This connection between the practical sanctifying work of the Spirit in our inner life, and His comes out very clearly in our context. ` If by the Spirit ye make to die the deeds of the body,ye shall live,' we read in 8:13. Then follows immediately, 'For as many as are led by the Spirit of God are sons of God.' That is, as many as allow they to be led by Him in this mortifying of the a the body, these are the sons of God. Th Spirit is the Spirit of the holy life which the and is in Christ Jesus, and which works in Divine life-power. He is the Spirit of Holiness only as such will He lead. Through Him God works in us both to will and to do of His good pleasure through Him God makes us perfect in every good work to do His will, working in us that which is well-pleasing in His sight. To be led of the Spirit implies in the first place the surrender to His work as He convinces of sin and cleanses soul and body for His temple. It is as the Indwelling Spirit, filling, sanctifying, and ruling the heart and life, that He enlightens and leads.

In the study of what the leading of the Spirit means, it is of the first importance to grasp this thought in all its bearings. It is only the spiritual mind that can discern spiritual things, and can receive the leadings of the Spirit. The mind must grow spiritual to become capable of spiritual guidance. Paul said to the Corinthians, that because, though born again, they were still carnal, as babes in Christ, he had not been able to teach them spiritual truth. If this holds of the teaching that comes through man, how much more of that direct teaching of the Spirit, by which He leads into all truth. The deepest mysteries of Scripture, as far as they are apprehended by human thought, can be studied and accepted and even taught by the unsanctified mind. But the leading of the Spirit, we cannot repeat it too often, does not begin in the region of thought or feeling. Deeper down, in the life itself, in the hidden laboratory of the inner life, whence issues the power that moulds the will and fashions the character in our spirits, there the Holy Spirit takes up His abode, there He breathes and moves and impels. He leads by inspiring us with a disposition out of which right purposes and come forth. 'That ye may be filled with the knowledge of His will in all wisdom and understanding:' that prayer teaches us that it is only to a spiritual understanding that the knowledge of God's will can be given. And the spiritual understanding only comes with the growth of the spiritual man, and the faithfulness to the spiritual life. He that would have the leading of Spirit must yield himself to have his life wholly possessed and filled of the Spirit. It was when Christ had been baptized with the Spirit that, 'being full of the Spirit, he was led by the Spirit in the wilderness (Luke 4: 1), 'that He returned in the power of the Spirit into Galilee' (4:14), and began His ministry in Nazareth with the words, ` The Spirit of the Lord is upon Me.'

All leading implies following. It is easily understood that to enjoy the leading of the Spirit demands a very teachable, "followsome" mind. The Spirit is not only hindered by the flesh as the power that commits sin, but still more by the flesh power that seeks to serve God. To be able to discern the Spirit's teaching, Scripture tells us that the ear must be circumcised, in a circumcision not made with hands, in the putting off of the body of the flesh, in the circumcision of Christ. The will and wisdom of the flesh must be feared and crucified, and denied. The ear must be closed to all that the flesh and its wisdom, whether in self or in men around us, has to say. In all our thoughts of God or our study of His Word, in all our drawings nigh to worship, and all our goings out to work for

Him, there must be a continued distrust and abnegation of self, and a very definite waiting on God by the Holy Spirit to teach and lead us. A soul that thus daily and hourly waits for a Divine leading, for the light of knowledge and of duty, will assuredly receive it. Would you be led of the, Spirit,give up, day by day, not only your will and wisdom, but your whole life and being. The Fire will descend and consume the sacrifice.

This leading of the Spirit must very specially be a thing of faith, and that in two senses. The beginning of the leading will come when we learn in holy fear to cultivate and act upon the confidence the Holy Spirit is in me, and is doing His work.

The Spirit's indwelling is the crowning piece of God's redemption work : the most spiritual and mysterious part of the mystery of godliness. Here,if anywhere, faith is needed. Faith is the faculty of the soul which recognizes the Unseen, the Divine; which receives the impression of the Divine Presence when God draws near; which in its measure accepts of what the Divine Being brings and gives to us. In the Holy Spirit is the most intimate communication of the Divine Life; here faith may not judge by what it feels or understands, but simply submits to God to let Him do what He has said. It meditates and worships, it prays and trusts ever afresh, it yields the whole soul in adoring acceptance and thanksgiving to the Savior's word, ' He shall be in you.' It in the assurance: the Holy Spirit, the Power of God, dwells within; in His own may depend upon it, He will lead me.

And then, with this more general faith indwelling of the Spirit, faith has also exercised in regard to each part of the leading. When there is a question I have laid before the Lord, and my soul has in simplicity and emptiness waited for His exposition and application of what in Word or Providence has met me, I must in faith trust my God that His guidance is not withheld. As we have said before, not in sudden impulses or strong impressions, not in heavenly voices or in remarkable interpositions, must we expect the ordinary leading of the Spirit. There are souls to whom such leading undoubtedly is given; time may come, as our nature becomes spiritual and lives more in direct contact with the Invisible, that our very thoughts and feeling become the conscious vehicles of His blessed voice. But this we must leave to Him, and the growth of our spiritual capacity. The lower steps of the ladder are let down low enough for the weakest to reach; God means every child of His to be led by the Spirit every day. Begin the path of following the Spirit's leading by believing, not only that the Spirit is within you, but that He, if hitherto you have little sought or enjoyed the wondrous blessing, does now at once undertake the work for which you ask and trust Him. Yield yourself to God in undivided surrender: believe with implicit confidence that

God's acceptance of the surrender means that you are given in charge of the Spirit. Through Him Jesus guides and rules and saves you.

But are we not in danger of being led away by the imaginings of our own hearts, and counting as leading of the Spirit what proves to be a delusion of the flesh ? And if so, where is our safeguard against such error ? The answer ordinarily given to this last question is: The Word of God. And yet that answer is but half the truth. Far too many have opposed to the danger of fanaticism the word of God, as interpreted by human reason or by the Church, and have erred no less than those they sought to oppose. The answer is: The word of God as taught by the Spirit of God. It is in the perfect harmony of the two that our safety is to be found. Let us on the one hand remember, that as all the word of God is given by the Spirit of God, so each word must be interpreted to us by that same Spirit. That this interpretation comes not from the Spirit above us or around us, suggesting thoughts to us, but from the indwelling Spirit, we need hardly repeat; it is only the spiritual man, whose inner life is under the dominion of the Spirit, who can discern,the spiritual meaning of the word. Let us on the other hold fast, that as all the word is given by the Spirit, so His great work is to honor that Word, and to unfold the fullness of Divine truth treasured there. Not in the Spirit without or with but little of the word; not in the word without or with but little of the Spirit; but in the word and Spirit both dwelling richly within us, and both yielded to in implicit obedience, is our assurance of safety in the path of the guidance.

This brings us back to the lesson we urged at the commencement: the leading of the Spirit is inseparable from the sanctifying of the Spirit each one who would be led of the Spirit begin by giving himself to be led-- of the word as far as he knows it. Begin at the beginning: obey the commandments. ` He that will do, shall know, said Jesus. ` Keep my commandments, and the Father will send you the Spirit.' Give up every sin. Give up in everything to the voice of conscience. Give up in everything to God, and let Him have His way. Through the Spirit mortify the deeds the body (v. 13). As a son of God place yourself at the entire disposal of the Spirit, to follow where He leads (v. 14). And the Spirit Himself, this same Spirit, through whom you mortify sin: and yield yourself to be led as a son, will bear witness with your spirit, in a joy and power hitherto unknown, that you are indeed a child of God enjoying all a child's privileges in his Father's love and guidance.

Blessed Father! I thank Thee for the message that as many as are led by the Spirit of God are the children of God. Thou wouldest not have Thy children guided by any one less than Thy own Holy Spirit. As He dwelt in Thy Son, and led Him, so He leads us too with a Divine and most blessed leading.

Father, Thou knowest how by reason of our not rightly knowing and not perfectly following this holy guidance, we are often unable to know His voice, so that the thought of the leading of the Spirit is more a burden than a joy. Father, forgive us. Be pleased graciously so to quicken our faith in the simplicity and certainty of the leading of the Spirit, that with our whole heart we may yield ourselves henceforth to walk in it.

Father, I do here yield myself to Thee as Thy child, in everything to be led of Thy Spirit. My own wisdom, my own will, my own way I forsake. Daily would I wait in deep dependence on a guidance from above. May my spirit ever be hushed in silence before Thy Holy Presence, while I wait to let Him rule within. As I through the Spirit make dead the deeds of the body, may I be transformed by the renewing of my mind to know Thy good and perfect will. May my whole being so be under the rule of the Indwelling, Sanctifying Spirit, that the spiritual understanding of Thy will may indeed be the rule of my life. Amen.

Chapter 20
The Spirit of Prayer

In like manner the Spirit also helpeth our infirmity - for we know not how to pray as we ought but the Spirit Himself maketh intercession for us with groanings that cannot be uttered; and He that searcheth the hearts knoweth what is the mind of the Spirit, because He maketh intercession for the saints according to God.' Romans. 8:26, 27.

Of the offices of the Holy Spirit, one that leads us most deeply into the understanding of His place in the Divine economy of grace, and into the mystery of the Holy Trinity, is the work He does as the Spirit of prayer. We have the Father to whom we pray, and who hears prayer. We have the Son through whom we pray, and through whom, in union with whom, we receive and really appropriate the answer. And we have the Holy Spirit in whom we pray, who prays in us according to the will of God, with such deeply hidden, unutterable sighings, that God has to search the hearts to know what is the mind of the Spirit. Just as wonderful and real as is the Divine work of God on the Throne, graciously hearing, and, by his,-mighty power, effectually answering prayer; just as Divine as is the work of the Son interceding and securing and transmitting the answer from above, is the work of the Holy Spirit in us in the prayer which waits and obtains the answer. The intercession within is as Divine as the intercession above. Let us try and understand why this should be so, and what it teaches.

In the creation of the world we see how it was the work of the Spirit to put Himself into contact with the dark and lifeless matter of chaos, and by His quickening energy to impart to it the power of life and fruitfulness. It was only after it had been thus vitalized by Him, that the Word of God gave it form, and called forth all the different types of life and beauty we now see. So, too, again in the creation of man it was the Spirit that was breathed into the body that had been formed from the ground, and that thus united itself with what would otherwise be dead matter. Even so, in the person of Jesus it is the Spirit through whose work a body was prepared for Him, through whom His body again was quickened from the grave, as it is through Him that our bodies are the temples of God, and the very members of our body the members of Christ. We think of the

Spirit in connection with the spiritual nature of the Divine Being, far removed from the grossness and feebleness of matter; we forget that it is the very work of the Spirit specially to unite Himself with what is material, to lift it up into Its own Spirit nature, and so to develop what will be the highest type of perfection, a spiritual body.

This view of the Spirit's work is essential to the understanding of the place He takes in the Divine work of redemption. In each part of that work there is a special place assigned to each of the Three Persons of the Holy Trinity. In the Father we have the unseen God, the Author of all. In the Son God revealed, made manifest, and brought nigh, He is the Form of God. In the Spirit of God we have the Indwelling God- the Power of God dwelling in human body and working in it what the Father and the Son have for us. The weakness and humiliation, yea, the very grossness of the flesh is the sphere for the operation of the Holy Spirit. Not only in the individual, but in the Church as a whole, what the Father has purposed, and the Son has procured, can be appropriated and take effect in the members of Christ who are still here in the flesh, only through the continual intervention and active operation of the Holy Spirit.

This is specially true of intercessory prayer. The coming of the kingdom of God, the increase of grace and knowledge and holiness in believers, their growing devotion to God's work and power for that work, the effectual working of God's power on the unconverted through the means of grace,--all this waits to come to us from God through Christ. But it cannot come except as it is looked for and desired, asked and expected, believed and hoped for. And this is now the wonderful position the Holy Ghost occupies, that to Him has been assigned the task of preparing the body of Christ to reach out and receive and hold fast what has been provided in the fullness of Christ the Head. For the communication of the Father's love and blessing, the Son and the Spirit must both work. The Son receives from the Father, reveals and brings nigh, as it were, descends from above; the Spirit from within wakens the soul to come out and meet its Lord. As indispensable as the unceasing intercession of Christ above, asking and receiving from the Father, is the unceasing intercession of the Spirit within, asking and accepting from the Son what the Father gives.

Very wonderful is the light that is cast upon this holy mystery by the words of our text. In the life of faith and prayer there are operations of the Spirit in which the word of God is made clear to our understanding, and our faith knows to express what it needs and asks. But there are also operations of the Spirit, deeper down than thoughts or feelings, where He works desires and yearnings in our spirit, in the secret springs of life and being, which God only can discover and understand. Of this nature is the real thirst for God Himself, the Living God, the longing to know the love 'that passeth knowledge,' and to be 'filled with all the fullness of God,' the hope in 'Him who is able to do exceeding abundantly above all we can ask or think,' even 'what hath not entered the heart of man to conceive.' When these aspirations indeed take possession of us, we begin to pray for what cannot be expressed, and our only comfort is then that the Spirit prays with His unutterable yearnings in a region and a language which the Heart Searcher alone knows and understands.

To the Corinthians Paul says, ' I will pray with the spirit, and I will pray with the understanding also.' Under the influence of the moving of the Holy Spirit and His miraculous gifts, their danger was to neglect the understanding. Our danger in these latter days is in the opposite direction: to pray with the understanding is easy and universal. We need to be reminded that, with the prayer with the understanding, there must come the prayer with the Spirit, the 'praying in the Holy Spirit' (Jude ver.20; Ephesians 6:18). We need to give its due place to each of the twofold operations of the Spirit. God's Word must dwell in us richly; our faith must seek to hold it clearly and intelligently, and to plead it in prayer. To have the words of Christ abiding in us, filling life and conduct, is one of the secrets of acceptable prayer. And yet we must always remember that in the inner sanctuary of our being, in the region of the unutterable and inconceivable (1 Cor.2:6), the Spirit prays for us what we do not know and cannot express. As we grow in the apprehension of the divinity of that Holy Spirit who dwells within, and the reality of His breathing within us, we shall recognize how infinitely beyond the conceptions of our mind must be that Divine hunger with which He draws us heavenward. We shall feel the need of cultivating not only the activity of faith, which seeks to grasp and obey God's word, and from that to learn to pray, but its deep passivity too. As we pray we shall remember how infinitely above our conception is God and the spirit-world into which by prayer we enter. Let us believe and rejoice that where heart and flesh fail, there God is the strength of our heart, there His Holy Spirit within us in the inmost sanctuary of our spirit, within the veil, does His unceasing work of intercession, and prays according to God within us. As we pray, let us at times worship in holy stillness, and yield ourselves to that Blessed Paraclete, who alone, who truly is, the Spirit of Supplication.'

'Because He maketh intercession for the saints.' Why does the apostle not say for us ; as he had said, 'We know not how to pray as we ought'? The expression, the saints, is a favourite one with Paul, where he thinks of the Church, either in one country or throughout the world. It is the special work of the Spirit, as dwelling in every member, to make the body realize its unity. As selfishness disappears, and the believer becomes more truly spiritual-minded,and he feels himself more identified with the body as a whole, he sees how its health and prosperity will be his own, and he learns what it is to 'pray at all seasons in the Spirit, watching thereunto in all perseverance for all saints.' It is as we give up ourselves to this work, in a large heartedness which takes in all the Church of God, that the Spirit will have free scope and will delight to do His work of intercession for the saints in us. It is specially in intercessory prayer that we may count upon the deep, unutterable, but all-prevailing intercession of the Spirit.

What a privilege ! to be the temple out of which the Holy Spirit cries to the Father His unceasing Abba! and offers His unutterable intercession, too deep for words. What blessedness! that as the Eternal Son dwelt in the flesh in Jesus of Nazareth, and prayed to the Father as man, that even so the Eternal Spirit should dwell in us, sinful flesh, to train us to speak with the Father even -as the Son did. Who would not yield himself to this blessed Spirit, to be made fit to take a share in that mighty Intercession work through which alone the Kingdom of God can be revealed ? The path is open, and invites all. Let the Holy Spirit have complete possession. Let Him fill you. Let Him be your life. Believe in the possibility of His making your very personality and consciousness the seat of His inbeing. Believe in the certainty of His working, and praying in you in a way that no human mind can apprehend. Believe that in the secrecy and apparent weakness and slowness of that work, His Divine Almighty Power is perfecting the Divine purpose and the Divine Oneness with your blessed Lord. And live as one in whom the things that pass all understanding have become Truth and Life, in whom the Intercession of the Spirit is part of your daily life in Christ.

Most Holy God! once more I bow in lowly adoration in Thy Presence, to thank Thee for the precious privilege of prayer. And specially would I thank Thee for the Grace that has not only given us in Thy Son the Intercessor above, but in Thy Spirit the Intercessor within. 0 my Father! Thou knowest that I can scarce take in the wondrous thought, that Thy Holy Spirit in very deed dwelleth in me, and prays in my feeble prayers. I do beseech Thee, discover to me all that hinders His taking full possession of me, and filling me with the consciousness of His Presence. Let my inmost being and my outer life all be so under His leading, that I may have the spiritual understanding that knows to ask according to Thy will, and the living faith that receives what it asks. And when I know not what or how to pray, 0 Father, teach me to bow in silent worship, and keep waiting before Thee, knowing that He breathes the wordless prayer which Thou alone canst understand.

Blessed God ! I am a temple of the Holy Spirit. I yield myself for Him to use me as the Spirit of Intercession. May my whole heart be so filled with the longing for Christ's honor, and His love for the lost, that my life may become one unutterable cry for the coming of Thy Kingdom. Amen.

Chapter 21
The Holy Spirit and Conscience.

'I say the truth in Christ, I lie not, my conscience also bearing me witness in the Holy Ghost.' Romans. 9:1.

'The Spirit Himself beareth witness with our spirit.' Romans 8:16.

God's highest glory is His Holiness in virtue of which He hates and destroys the evil, loves and works the good. In man, conscience has the same work: it condemns sin and approves the right. Conscience is the remains of God's image in man, the nearest approach to the Divine in him, the guardian of God's honour amid the ruin of the fall. As a consequence, God's work of redemption must always begin with conscience. The Spirit of God is the Spirit of His Holiness ; conscience is a spark of the Divine holiness; harmony between the work of the Holy Spirit in, renewing and sanctifying man, and the work of conscience, is most intimate and essential. The believer who would be filled with the Holy Spirit, and experience to the full the blessings He has to give, must in the first place see to it that he yields to conscience the place and the honour which belong to it. Faithfulness to conscience is the first step in the path of restoration to the Holiness of God. Intense conscientiousness will be the groundwork and characteristic of true spirituality. As it is the work of conscience to witness to our being right towards our sense of duty and towards God, and the work of the Spirit to witness to God's acceptance of our faith in Christ and our obedience to Him, the testimony of the Spirit and of conscience will, as the Christian life progresses, become increasingly identical. We shall feel the need and the blessedness of saying with Paul, in regard to all our conduct: 'My conscience also bearing me witness in the Holy Ghost.'

Conscience can be compared to the window of a room, through which the light of heaven shines into it, and through which we can look out and see that heaven, with all that its light shines on. The heart is the chamber in which our Life dwells, our Ego, or Soul, with its powers and affections. On the walls of that chamber there is written the law of God. Even in the heathen it is still partly legible, though sadly darkened and defaced. 'In the believer the law is written anew by the Holy Spirit, in letters of light, which often at first are but dim, but grow clearer and glow brighter as they are freely exposed to the action of the light without. With every sin I commit, the light that shines in makes it manifest and condemns it. If the sin be not confessed and forsaken, the stain remains, and conscience becomes defiled, because the mind refused the teaching of the light (Tit. 1:15). And so with one sin after another the window gets darker and darker, until the light can hardly shine through at all, and the Christian can sin on undisturbed, with a conscience to a large extent blinded and without feeling. In His work of renewal the Holy Spirit does not create new faculties: He renews and sanctifies those already existing. Conscience is the work of the Spirit of God the Creator; the first care of the Spirit of God the Redeemer is to restore what sin has defiled. It is only by restoring conscience to full and healthy action, and revealing in it the wonderful grace of Christ, 'the Spirit bearing witness with our spirit,' that He enables the believer to live a life in the full light of God's favour. It is as the window of the heart that looks heavenward is cleansed and kept clean that we can walk in the Light.

The work of the Spirit on conscience is a threefold one. Through conscience the Spirit causes the light of God's holy law to shine into the heart. A room may have its curtains drawn, and even its shutters closed: this cannot prevent the lightning flash from time to time shining into the darkness. Conscience may be so sin-stained and seared that the strong man within dwells in perfect peace. When the lightning from Sinai flashes into the heart, conscience wakens up, and is at once ready to admit and sustain the condemnation. Both the law and the gospel, with their call to repentance and their conviction of sin, appeal to conscience. And it is not till conscience has said Amen to the charge of transgression and unbelief that deliverance can truly come.

It is through conscience that the Spirit likewise causes the light of mercy to shine. When the windows of a house are stained, they need to be washed. How much more shall the blood of Christ cleanse your conscience! The whole aim of the precious, blood of Christ is to reach the conscience, to silence its accusations, and cleanse it, till it testify: Every stain is removed; the love of the Father streams in Christ in unclouded brightness into my soul. 'A heart sprinkled from an evil conscience,' 'having no more conscience of sin' (Heb. 9:14, 10:2, 22), is meant to be the privilege of every believer. It becomes so when conscience learns to say Amen to God's message of the Power of Jesus' Blood.

The conscience that has been cleansed in the blood must be kept clean by a walk in the obedience of faith, with the light of God's favor shining on it. To the promise of the Indwelling Spirit, and His engagement to lead in all God's will, conscience must say its Amen too, and testify that He does it. The believer is called to walk in humble tenderness and watchfulness, lest in anything, even the least, conscience should accuse him for not having done what he knew to be right, or done what was not of faith. He may be content with nothing less than Paul's joyful testimony, I Our glorying is this, the testimony of our conscience, that in holiness and godly sincerity, by the grace of God, we behaved ourselves in the world' (2 Cor. 1:12. Comp. Acts 23:1, 24: 16 ; 2 Tim. 1: 3). Let us note these words well: 'Our glorying is this, the testimony of our conscience! It is as the window is kept clean and bright by our abiding in the light, that we can have fellowship with the Father and the Son, the love of heaven shining in unclouded, and our love rising up in childlike trustfulness. 'Beloved! if our heart condemn us not, we have boldness toward God, because we keep His commandments, and do those things that are pleasing in His sight' (1 John 3: 21,22).

The maintenance of a good conscience toward God from day to day is essential to the life of faith. The believer must aim at, must be satisfied with, nothing less than this. He may be assured that it is within his reach. The believers in the Old Testament by faith had the witness that they pleased God (Heb. 11: 4, 5, 6, 39). In the New Testament it is set before us, not only as a command to be obeyed, but as a grace to be wrought by God Himself. 'That ye might walk worthy of the Lord unto all well-pleasing, strengthened with all might according to His glorious power.' ' May God fulfill all the good pleasure of His goodness, and the work of faith with power.' ' Working in us that which is well-pleasing in His sight! (Col.1:10,11; 2 Thess.1:11; 1 Thess.4:1; Heb.12:28, 13:21).

The more we seek this testimony of conscience that we are doing what is well-pleasing to God, the more shall we feel the liberty, with every failure that surprises us, to look at once to the blood that ever cleanses, and the stronger will be our assurance that the indwelling sinfulness, and all its workings that are yet unknown to us, are covered by that blood too. The blood that has sprinkled the conscience abides and acts there in the power of the Eternal Life that knows no intermission, and of the unchangeable Priesthood that saves completely. 'If we walk in the light, as He is in the light, we have fellowship one with another, and the blood of Jesus Christ cleanseth us from all sin."

The cause of the feebleness of our faith is owing to nothing so much as the want of a clean conscience. Mark well how closely Paul connects them in 1 Tim.: 'Love out of a pure heart, and a good conscience, and faith unfeigned' (1: 5). 'Holding faith and a good conscience, which some having thrust from them, have made shipwreck of the faith' (1:19). And especially (3: 9), ' Holding the mystery of -the faith in a pure conscience.' The conscience is the seat of faith. He that would grow strong in faith, and have boldness with God, must know that he is pleasing Him (1 John 3: 21, 22). Jesus said most distinctly that it is for those who love Him and keep His commandments, that the promise of the Spirit, with the indwelling of the Father and the Son, the abiding in His love, and power in prayer, is meant.

How can we confidently claim these promises, unless in childlike simplicity our conscience can testify that we fulfill the conditions ? Oh, ere the Church can rise to the height of her holy calling as intercessor, and claim these unlimited promises as really within her reach, believers will have to draw nigh to their Father, glorying, like Paul, in the testimony of their conscience, that, by the Grace of God, they are walking in holiness and godly sincerity. It will have to be seen that this is the -deepest humility, and brings most glory to God's free grace, to give up man's ideas of what we can attain, and accept God's declaration of what He desires and promises, as the only standard of what we are to be.

And how is this blessed life to be attained, in which we can daily appeal to God and men with Paul: 'I say the truth in Christ, my conscience bearing me witness in the Holy Ghost'? The first step is: Bow very low under the reproofs of conscience. Be not content with the general confession that there is a great deal wrong. Beware of confounding actual transgression with the involuntary workings of the sinful nature. If the latter are to be conquered and made dead by the indwelling Spirit (Rom. viii. 13), you must first deal with the former. Begin with some single sin, and give conscience time in silent submission and humiliation to reprove and condemn. Say to your Father, that in this one thing you are, by His grace, going to obey. Accept anew Christ's wonderful offer to take entire possession of your heart, to dwell in you as Lord and Keeper. Trust Him by His Holy Spirit to do this, even when you feel weak and helpless. Remember that obedience, the taking and keeping Christ's words in your will and life, is the only way to prove the reality of your surrender to Him, or your interest in His work and grace. And vow in faith, that by God's Grace you will exercise yourself herein, 'always to have a conscience void of offense toward God and toward man.'

When you have begun this with one sin, proceed with others, step by step. As you are faithful in keeping conscience pure, the light will shine more brightly from heaven into the heart, discovering sin you had not noticed before, bringing out distinctly the law written by the Spirit you had not been able to read. Be willing to be taught ; be trustfully sure that the Spirit will teach. Every honest effort to keep the blood-cleansed conscience clean, in the light of God, will be met with the aid of the Spirit. Only yield yourself heartily and entirely to God's will, and to the power of His Holy Spirit.

As you thus bow to the reproofs of conscience, and give yourself wholly to do

God's will, your courage will grow strong that it is possible to have a conscience void of offense. The witness of conscience, as to what you are doing, and will do by grace, will be met by the witness of the Spirit as to what Christ is doing and will do. In childlike simplicity you will seek to begin each day with the simple prayer: Father! there is nothing now between Thee and Thy child. My conscience divinely cleansed in the blood, bears me witness, Father! let not even the shadow of a cloud intervene this day. In everything would I do Thy will: Thy Spirit dwells in me, and leads me, and makes me strong in Christ. And you will enter upon that life which glories in free grace alone when it says at the close of each day, 'Our glorying is this, the testimony of our conscience, that in holiness and godly sincerity, by the Grace of God, we have behaved ourselves in the world': 'My conscience bearing me witness in the Holy Ghost.'

Gracious God! I thank Thee for the voice Thou hast given in our heart, to testify whether we are pleasing to Thee or not. I thank Thee, that when that witness condemned me, with its terrible Amen to the curse of Thy law, Thou didst give the blood of Thy Son to cleanse the conscience. I thank Thee that at this moment my conscience can say Amen to the voice of the blood, and that I may look up to Thee in full assurance, with a heart cleansed from the evil conscience.

I thank Thee too for the Witness from heaven to what Jesus hath done and is doing for me and in me. I thank Thee that He glorifies Christ in me, gives me His Presence and His Power, and transforms me into His likeness. I thank Thee that to the presence and the work of Thy Spirit in my heart, my conscience can likewise say, Amen.

O my Father! I desire this day to walk before Thee with a good conscience, to do nothing that might grieve Thee or my Blessed Lord Jesus. I ask Thee, may, in the power of the Holy Spirit, the cleansing in the blood be a living, continual, and most effectual deliverance from the power of sin, binding and strengthening me to Thy perfect service. And may my whole walk with Thee be in the joy of the united witness of conscience and Thy Spirit that I am well-pleasing to Thee. Amen.

Chapter 22
The Revelation of the Spirit

My preaching was not in persuasive words of man's wisdom, but in demonstration of the Spirit and of power: that your faith should not stand in the wisdom of men, but in the power of God. Howbeit we speak wisdom among the perfect: yet a wisdom not of this world; but we speak God's wisdom in a mystery, even the wisdom that hath been hidden, which none of the rulers of this world knoweth. But unto us God revealed it through the Spirit. The things of God none knoweth, save the Spirit of God, But we received, not the spirit which in of the world, but the Spirit which is of God, that we might know the things which are freely given to us by God; which things also we speak, not in the word which man's wisdom teacheth, but which the Spirit teacheth. Now the natural man receiveth not the things of the Spirit of God. But he that is spiritual judgeth all things. 1 Corinthians 2:4-15.

In this passage Paul contrasts the spirit of the world and the Spirit of God. The point in which the contrast specially comes out is in the wisdom or knowledge of the truth. It was in seeking 'knowledge that man fell. It was in the pride of knowledge that heathenism had its origin; 'professing themselves to be wise, they became fools' (Rom. 1:22). It was in wisdom, philosophy, and the search after truth, that. the Greeks sought their glory. It was in the knowledge of God's will, the form of the knowledge and of the truth in the law' (Rom. 2:17-20), that the Jew made his boast. And yet when Christ, the wisdom of God, appeared on earth, Jew and Greek combined to reject Him. Man's wisdom, whether in possession of a revelation or not, is utterly insufficient for comprehending God or His wisdom. As his heart is alienated from God, so that he does not love or do His will, so his mind is darkened that he cannot know Him aright. Even when in Christ the light of God in its Divine love shone upon men, they knew it not, and saw no beauty in it.

In the Epistle to the Romans, Paul had dealt with man's trust in his own righteousness, and its insufficiency. To the Corinthians, especially in the first three chapters, he exposes the insufficiency of man's wisdom. And that not merely when it was a question of discovering God's truth and will, as with the

Greeks; but even where God had revealed it, as with the Jews, man was incapable of seeing it without a Divine illumination, the light of the Holy Spirit. The rulers of this world, Jew and Gentile, had crucified the Lord of glory because they knew not the wisdom of God. In writing to believers at Corinth, and warning them against the wisdom of the world, Paul is not dealing with any heresy, Jewish or heathen. He is speaking to believers, who had fully accepted his gospel of a crucified Christ, but who were in danger, in preaching or hearing the truth, to deal with it in the power of human wisdom. He reminds them that the truth of God, as a hidden spirit mystery, can only be apprehended by a spiritual revelation. The rejection of Christ by the Jews had been the great proof of the utter incapacity of human wisdom to grasp a Divine revelation, without the spiritual internal illumination of the Holy Spirit. The Jews prided themselves on their attachment to God's word, their study of it, their conformity to it in life and conduct. The issue proved that, without their being conscious of it, they utterly misunderstood it, and rejected the very Messiah whom they thought they were waiting for and trusting in. Divine revelation, as Paul expounds it in this chapter, means three things. God must make known in His word what He thinks and does. Every preacher who is to communicate the message, must not only be in possession of the truth, but continually be taught by the Spirit how to speak it. And every hearer needs the inward illumination: it is only as he is a spiritual man, with his life under the rule of the Spirit, that his mind can take in spiritual truth.

As we have the mind, the disposition of Christ, we can discern the truth as it is in Christ Jesus. This teaching is what the Church in our days, and each believer, specially needs. With the Reformation the insufficiency of man's righteousness, of his power really to fulfill God's law, obtained universal recognition in the Reformed Churches, and in theory at least is everywhere accepted among Evangelical Christians. The insufficiency of man's wisdom has by no means obtained as clear recognition. While the need of the Holy Spirit's teaching is, in a general way, willingly admitted, it will be found that neither in the teaching of the Church, nor in the lives of believers, has this blessed truth that practical and all-embracing supremacy without which the wisdom and the spirit of this world will still assert their power.

The proof of what we have said will be found in what Paul says of His own preaching: 'Our preaching was not in man's wisdom, but in the Spirit; that your faith might not stand in the wisdom of men, but in the power of God.' He is not writing, as to the Galatians, of two gospels, but of two ways of preaching the one gospel of Christ's cross. He says that to preach it in persuasive words of man's wisdom, produces a faith that will bear the mark of its origin ; it will stand in the wisdom of man. As long as it is nourished by men and means, it may stand and flourish. But it cannot stand alone or in the day of trial - A man may, with such preaching, become a believer, but will be a feeble believer. The faith, on the other hand, begotten of a preaching in the Spirit and power, stands in the power of God. The believer is led by the preaching, by the Holy Spirit Himself, past man, to direct contact with the living God: his faith stands in the power of God. As long as the state of the great majority of our church members, notwithstanding such an abundance of the means of grace, is so feeble and sickly, with so little of the faith that stands in the power of God, mighty to overcome the world, to purify the heart, and to do the greater works, we cannot but fear that it is because too much, even of our true gospel preaching, is more in the wisdom of man than in the demonstration of the Spirit and of power. If a change is to be effected both in the spirit in which our preachers and teachers speak, and our congregations listen and expect, it must commence, I am sure, in the personal life of the individual believer.

We must learn to fear our own wisdom. 'Trust in the Lord with thy whole heart, and lean not to thine own understanding.' Paul says, to believers: 'If any man thinketh that he is wise, let him become a fool, that he may be wise ' (I Cor.3:18). When Scripture tells us that 'they that are Christ's have crucified the flesh,' this includes the understanding of the flesh, the fleshly mind of which Scripture speaks. Just as in the crucifixion of self I give up my own goodness, my own strength, my own will to the death, because there is no good in it, and, look to Christ by the power of His life to give me the goodness, and the strength, and the will which is pleasing to God, so it must be very specially with my wisdom Man's mind is one of his noblest and most God-like faculties, But sin rules over it and in it. A man may be truly converted, and yet not know to what an extent it is his natural mind with which he is trying to grasp and hold the truth of God. The reason that there is so much Bible reading and teaching which has no power to elevate and sanctify the life is simply this: it is not truth which has been revealed and received through the Holy Spirit.

This holds good, too, of truth which has once been taught us by the Holy Spirit, but which, having been lodged in the understanding, is now held simply, by the memory.' Manna speedily loses its heavenliness, when stored up on earth. Truth received from heaven loses its Divine freshness, unless there every day be the anointing with fresh oil. The believer needs, day by day, hour by hour, to feel that there is nothing in which the power of the flesh, of nature, can assert itself more insidiously, than in the activity of the mind or reason in its dealing with the Divine word. This will make him feel that he must continually seek, in Paul's language, 'to become a fool.' He needs, each time he has to do with God's word, or thinks of God's truth, in faith and teachableness, to wait for the promised teaching of the Spirit. He needs ever again to ask for the circumcised ear: the ear in which the fleshly power of the understanding has been removed, and in which the spirit of the life in Christ Jesus within the heart listens in the obedience of the life, even as Christ did. To such the word will be fulfilled : 'I thank Thee, Father, that Thou hast hid these things from the wise and prudent, and hast revealed them unto babes.'

The lesson for all ministers and teachers, all professors and theologians, all students and readers of the Bible, is one of deep and searching solemnity. Have we felt, have we even sought to feel, that there must be perfect correspondence between the objective spiritual contents of the revelation, and the subjective spiritual apprehension of it on our part ? between our apprehension of it and our communication of it, both in the power of the Holy Spirit ? between our communication of it, and the reception by those to whom we bring it ? Would God that over our theological halls and our training institutes, over the studies of our commentators and writers, our ministers and teachers, there were written those words of Paul: 'The things of God none knoweth, save the Spirit of God : unto us God revealed them through the Spirit.' Would that our ministers could influence and train their congregations to see, that not the amount, or the clearness, or the interest of the Bible knowledge received will decide the blessing and the power that it brings, but the measure of real dependence on the Holy Spirit. 'Them that honour Me. I will honour:' nowhere will this word be found more true than here. The crucifixion of self and all its wisdom, the coming in weakness, and in fear, and in much trembling, as Paul did, will most assuredly be met from above with the demonstration Of the Spirit and of power.

Believer ! it is not enough that the light of Christ shines on you in the Word, the light of the Spirit must shine in you. Each time you come to the word, in study, in hearing a sermon, or reading a religious book, there ought to be, as distinct as your intercourse with the external means, a definite act of self -abnegation, denying your own wisdom, and. yielding yourself in faith to the Divine Teacher. Believe very distinctly that He dwells within you. He seeks the mastery, the sanctification of your inner life, in entire surrender and obedience to Jesus. Rejoice to renew your surrender to Him. Reject the spirit of the world which is still in you, with its wisdom and self - confidence; come, in poverty of spirit, to be led by the Spirit that is of God. 'Be not fashioned according to the world,' with its confidence in the flesh, and self, and its wisdom; 'but be ye transformed by the renewing of your mind, that ye may prove what is the good, and perfect, and acceptable will of God.' It is a transformed, renewed life, that, only wants to know God's perfect will, that will be taught by the Spirit. Cease from your own wisdom; wait for the wisdom in the inward parts which God has promised: you will increasingly be able to testify of the things which have not entered into the hearts of men to conceive: 'God hath revealed them to us by His Spirit.'

O God! I bless Thee for the wondrous revelation of Thyself in Christ crucified, the wisdom of God, and the power of God. I bless Thee, that while man's wisdom leaves him helpless in presence of the power of sin, and death, Christ crucified proves that He is the wisdom of God by the mighty redemption He works as the power of God. And I bless Thee, that what he wrought and bestows as an Almighty Savior is revealed within us by the Divine light of Thine Own Holy Spirit.

O Lord! we beseech Thee, teach Thy Church that wherever Christ, as the power of God, is not manifested, it is because He is so little known as the wisdom. of God, in the light in which the indwelling Spirit alone reveals Him. Oh! teach Thy Church to lead each child of God to the personal teaching and revelation of Christ within.

Show us, O God ! that the one great hindrance is our own wisdom, our imagination that we can understand the Word and Truth of God. Oh! teach us to become fools that we may be wise. May our 'whole life become one continued act of faith, that the Holy Spirit will surely do His work of teaching, guiding and leading into the truth. Father ! Thou gavest Him that He might reveal Jesus in His glory within us ; we wait for this. Amen.

Chapter 23
Spiritual or Carnal.

And I, brethren, could not speak unto you as unto spiritual, but as unto carnal, as unto babes in Christ. I fed you with milk, not with meat; for ye were not Yet able to bear it; nay, not even now are ye able; for whereas there is among you jealousy and strife, are ye not carnal, and walk after the manner of men?' I Corinthians 3:1-3

In the previous Chapter the Apostle had contrasted the believer as spiritual, with the unregenerate as the natural (Or Psychical) man: the man of the Spirit with the man of the soul (1 Cor.2:14, 15). Here he supplements that teaching. He tells the Corinthians that, though they, have the Spirit, he cannot call them spiritual; that epithet belongs to those who have not only received the Spirit, but have yielded themselves to Him to possess and rule their whole life. Those who have not done this, in whom the power of the flesh is still more manifest than that of the Spirit, must be called not spiritual, but fleshly or carnal. There are thus three states in which a man may be found. The unregenerate is still the natural man, not having the Spirit of God. The regenerate, who is still a babe in Christ, whether because he is only lately converted, or because he has stood still and not advanced, is the carnal man, giving way to the power of the flesh. The believer in whom the Spirit has obtained full supremacy, is the spiritual man. The whole passage is suggestive of rich instruction in regard to the life of the Spirit within us.

The young Christian is still carnal. Regeneration is a birth: the center and root of the personality, the spirit, has been renewed and taken possession of by the Spirit of God. But time is needed for its power from that center to extend through all the circumference of our being. The kingdom of God is like unto a seed; the life in Christ is a growth; and it would be against the laws of nature and grace alike if we expected from the babe in Christ the strength that can only be found in the young men, or the rich experience of the fathers. Even where in the young convert there is great singleness of heart and faith, with true love and devotion to the Saviour, time is needed for a deeper knowledge of self and sin, for a spiritual insight into what God's will and grace are. With the young believer it is not unnatural that the emotions are deeply stirred, and that the mind delights in the contemplation of Divine truth; with the growth in grace, the will becomes the more important thing, and the waiting for the Spirit's power in the life and character more than the delight in those thoughts and images of the life which alone the mind could give. We need not wonder if the babe in Christ is still carnal.

Many Christians remain carnal. God has not only called us to grow, but has provided all the conditions and powers needful for growth. And yet it is, sadly true, that there are many Christians who, like the Corinthians, remain babes in Christ when they ought to be going on to perfection, 'attaining unto a full-grown man.' In some cases the blame is almost more with the Church and its teaching, than with the individuals themselves. When the preaching makes salvation chiefly to consist in pardon and peace and the hope of heaven, or when, if a holy life be preached, the truth of Christ our Sanctification, our Sufficient Strength to be holy, and the Holy Spirit's indwelling, be not taught clearly and in the power of the Spirit, growth can hardly be expected: Ignorance, human and defective views of the gospel, as the power of God unto a, present salvation in sanctification, are the cause of the evil.

In other cases the root of the evil is to be found in the unwillingness of the Christian to deny self and crucify the flesh. The call of Jesus to every disciple is,'If any man will come after Me, let him deny himself.' The Spirit is only given to the obedient; He can only do His work in those who are willing absolutely to give up self to the death.

The sin that proved that the Corinthians were carnal was their jealousy and strife. When Christians are not willing to give up the sin of selfishness and temper; when, whether in the home relationship or in the wider circle of church and public life, they want to retain the liberty of giving way to, or excusing evil feelings, of pronouncing their own judgments, and speaking words that are not in perfect love, then they remain carnal. With all their knowledge, and their enjoyment of religious ordinances, and their work for God's kingdom, they are carnal and not spiritual. They grieve the Holy Spirit of God; they cannot have the testimony that they are pleasing to God. God is Love: if we would not be carnal, let us love. 'Above all things, put on love, which is the bond of perfectness.'

The carnal Christian cannot apprehend spiritual truth. Paul writes to these Corinthians: 'I fed you with milk, and not with meat; for ye were not able to bear it; nay, not even now are ye able.' The Corinthians prided themselves on their wisdom; Paul thanked God that they were 'enriched in all knowledge.' There was nothing in His teaching that they would not have been able to comprehend with the understanding. But the real spiritual entering into the truth in power, so as to possess it and be possessed by it, so as to have not only the thoughts but the very thing the words speak of, this the Holy Spirit only can give. And He gives it only in the spiritually-minded man. The teaching and leading of the Spirit is given to the obedient, is preceded by the dominion of the Spirit in mortifying the deeds of the body (see Rom.8: 13 and 14). Spiritual knowledge is not deep thought, but living contact, entering into and being united to the truth as it is in Jesus, a spiritual reality, a substantial existence. 'The Spirit teacheth, combining spiritual things with spiritual;' into a spiritual mind He works spiritual truth. It is not the power of intellect, it is not even the earnest desire to know the truth, that fits a man for the Spirit's teaching; it is a life yielded to Him in waiting dependence and full obedience to be made spiritual, that receives the spiritual wisdom and understanding. In the mind (nous, in the Scripture meaning of the term) these two elements, the moral and the cognitive, are united; only as the former has precedence and sway, can the latter apprehend what God has spoken.

It is easy to understand how a carnal or fleshly life with its walk, and the fleshly mind with its knowledge, act and react on each other. As far as we are giving way to the flesh, we are incapable of receiving spiritual insight into truth. We may 'know all mysteries, and have all knowledge,'without love, the love which the Spirit works in the inner life; it is only a knowledge that puffeth up, it profiteth nothing. The carnal life makes the knowledge carnal. And this knowledge again, being thus held in the fleshly mind, strengthens the religion of the flesh, of self-trust and self effort; the truth so received has no power to renew and make free. No wonder that there is so much Bible teaching and Bible knowledge, with so little of real spiritual result in a life of holiness. Would God that His word might sound through His Church: 'Whereas there is among you jealousy and strife, are ye not carnal?' Unless we be living spiritual lives, full of humility, and love, and self-sacrifice, spiritual truth, the truth of God, cannot enter or profit us. Love alone is light: want of love is darkness (1 John 2:9).

Every Christian is called of God to be a spiritual man. Paul reproves these Corinthians, only but a few years since brought out of gross heathenism, that they are not yet spiritual. The great redemption in Christ had this most distinctly as its object, the removal of every hindrance, that the Spirit of God might be able to make man's heart and life a worthy home for God who is a Spirit. That redemption was no failure; the Holy Spirit came down to inaugurate a new, before unknown, dispensation of indwelling life and power. The promise and the love of the Father, the power and the glory of the Son, the presence of the Spirit on earth all are pledge and guarantee that it can be. As sure as the natural man can become a regenerate man, can a regenerate man, who is still carnal, become spiritual.

And why is it not so? The question brings us into the presence of that strange and unfathomable mystery-the power God has given men of accepting or refusing His offers, of being true or being unfaithful to the grace He has given. We have already spoken of that unfaithfulness on the part of the Church, in its defective teaching of the indwelling and the sanctifying power of the Holy Spirit in the believer, and on the part of believers in their unwillingness to forsake all to let the Holy Spirit get entire possession, and do a perfect work in them. Let us here rather seek, once again, to gather up what Scripture teaches as to the way to become spiritual.

It is the Holy Spirit who makes the spiritual man. He alone can do it. He does it most certainly where the whole man is yielded up to Him. To have the whole being pervaded, influenced, sanctified by the Holy Spirit; to have first our spirit, then the soul, with the will, the feelings, the mind, and so even the body, under His control, moved and guided by Him, this makes and marks the spiritual man.

The first step on the way to this is faith. We must seek the deep, living, absorbing conviction that there is a Holy Spirit in us; that He is the Mighty Power of God dwelling and working within; that He is the representative of Jesus, making Him present within us as our Redeemer King, mighty to save. In the union of a holy fear and trembling at the almost tremendous glory of this truth of an Indwelling God, with the childlike joy and trust of knowing Him to be the Paraclete, the Inbringer of the Divine and irrevocable presence of God and of Christ, this thought must become the inspiration of life: The Holy Spirit has His home within us: in our spirit is His hidden, blessed dwelling-place.

As we are filled with the faith of what He is and will do, and see that it is not done, we ask for the hindrance. We find that there is an opposing power, the flesh. From Scripture we learn how the flesh has its twofold action : from the flesh springs not only unrighteousness, but self-righteousness. Both must be confessed and surrendered to Him whom the Spirit would reveal and enthrone as Lord, our Mighty Savior. All that is carnal and sinful, all the works of the flesh, must be given up and cast out. But no less must all that is carnal, however religious it appears, all confidence in the flesh, all self-effort and self-struggling be rooted out. The soul, with its power, must be brought into the captivity and subjection of Jesus Christ. In deep and daily dependence on God must the Holy Spirit be accepted, waited for, and followed.

Thus walking in faith and obedience, we may count on the Holy Spirit to do a divine and most blessed work within us. 'If we live by the Spirit;' --this is the faith that is needed ; we believe that God, a Spirit dwells in us. Then follows: 'by the Spirit let us live;' this is the obedience that is asked. In the faith of that Holy Spirit who is in us, we know that we have sufficient strength to walk by the

Spirit, and yield ourselves to His mighty working, to work in us to will and to do all that is pleasing in God's sight.

Gracious God ! we humbly pray Thee to teach us all to profit by the solemn lessons of this portion of Thy blessed word.

Fill us with holy fear and trembling lest, with all our knowledge of the truth of Christ and the Spirit, we should be carnal in disposition and conduct, not walking in the love and purity of Thy Holy Spirit. May we understand that knowledge only puffeth up, unless it be under the rule of the love that buildeth up.

Give us to hear Thy call to all Thy children to be spiritual. It is Thy purpose, that even as with Thy beloved Son, their whole daily life, even in the very least things, should give evidence of being the fruit of Thy Spirit's indwelling. May we all accept the call, as from Thy love, inviting us to our highest blessedness, conformity to Thy likeness in Christ Jesus.

Chapter 24
The Temple of the Holy Spirit.

Know ye not that ye are the temple of God, and that the Spirit of God dwelleth in you ?' I Corinthians 3:16.

In using the illustration of the Temple as the type of God's dwelling in us by the Holy Spirit, Scripture invites us to study the analogy. The Temple was made in all things according to a pattern seen by Moses on the Mount, a shadow cast by the Eternal Spiritual Realities which it was to symbolize. One of these realities-for Divine Truth is exceeding rich and full and has many and very diverse applications-One of these realities shadowed forth by the Temple, is man's threefold nature. Because man was created in the image of God, the Temple is not only the setting forth of the mystery of man's approach into the presence of God, but equally of God's way of entering into man, to take up His abode with him.

We are familiar with the division of the Temple into three parts. There was its exterior, seen by all men, with the outer court, in to which every Israelite might enter, and where all the external religious service was performed. There was the Holy Place, into which alone the priests might enter, to present to God the blood or the incense, the bread or the oil, they had brought from without. But though near, they were still not within the veil; into the immediate presence of God they might not come. God dwelt in the Holiest of all,in a light inaccessible, where none might venture nigh. The momentary entering of the High Priest once a year was but to bring into full consciousness the truth that there was no place for man there, until the veil should have been rent and taken away.

Man is God's temple. In him, too, there are the three parts. In the body you have the outer court, the external visible life, where all the conduct has to be regulated by God's law, and where all the service consists in looking to that which is done without us and for us to bring us nigh to God. Then there is the soul, with its inner life, its power of mind and feeling and will. In the regenerate man this is the Holy Place, where thoughts and affections and desires move to and fro as the priests of the sanctuary, rendering God their service in the full light of consciousness. And then comes within the veil, hidden from all human sight and light, the hidden inmost sanctuary, ' the secret place of the Most High,' where God dwells, and where man may not enter, until the veil is rent at God's own bidding.

Man has not only body and soul, but also spirit. Deeper down than where the soul with its consciousness can enter, there is a spirit-nature linking man with God.

So fearful is sin's power, that in some this power is given up to death: they are sensual, not having the Spirit. In others, it is nothing more than a dormant power, a possibility waiting for the quickening of the Holy Spirit. In the believer it is the inner chamber of the heart, of which the Spirit has taken. possession, and from out of which He waits to do His glorious work, making soul and body holy to the Lord.

And yet this indwelling, unless where it is recognized, and yielded to, and humbly maintained in adoration and love, often brings comparatively little blessing. And the one great lesson which the truth that we are God's temple, because His Spirit dwells in us, must teach us, is this, to, acknowledge the Holy Presence that dwells within us. This alone will enable us to regard the whole temple, even to the outmost court, as sacred to His service, and to yield every power of our nature to His leading and will. The most sacred part of the Temple, that for which all the rest existed and on which all depended, was the Holiest of all. Even though the priests might never enter there, and might never see the glory that dwelt there, all their conduct was regulated, and all their faith animated, by the thought of the unseen Presence there. It was this that gave the sprinkling of the blood and the burning of the incense their value. It was this made it a privilege to draw nigh, and gave confidence to go out and bless. It was the Most Holy, the Holiest of all, that made the place of their serving to them a Holy Place. Their whole life was controlled and inspired by the faith of the unseen indwelling glory within the veil.

It is not otherwise with the believer. Until he learns by faith to tremble in presence of the wondrous mystery that he is God's temple, because God's Spirit dwelleth in him, he never will yield himself to his high vocation with the holy reverence or the joyful confidence that becomes him. As long as he looks only into the Holy Place, into the heart, as far as man can see and know what passes there, he will often search in vain for the Holy Spirit, or only find cause for bitter shame that his workings are so few and feeble. Each of us must learn to know that there is a Holiest of all in that temple which he himself is; the secret place of the Most High within us must become the central truth in our temple worship. This must be to us the meaning of our confession: 'I believe in the Holy Ghost.'

And how is this deep faith in the hidden indwelling to become ours ? Taking our stand, upon God's blessed Word, we must accept and appropriate its teaching. We must take trouble to believe that God means what it says. I am a temple ; just such a temple as God commanded to be built of old ; He meant me to see in it what I am to be. There the Holiest of all was the central point, the essential thing. It was all dark, secret, hidden,till the time of unveiling came. It demanded and received the faith of priest and people. The Holiest of all within me, too, is unseen and hidden, a thing for faith alone to know and deal with. Let me, as I approach to the Holy One, bow before Him in deep and lowly reverence. Let me there say that I believe what He says, that His Holy Spirit,

God, one with the Father and the Son, even now has His abode within me. I will meditate, and be still, until something of the overwhelming glory of the truth fall upon me, and faith begin to realize it: I am His temple, and in the secret place He sits upon His throne. As I yield myself in silent meditation and worship day by day, surrendering and setting open my whole being to Him, He will in His divine, loving, living power, shine into my consciousness the light of His presence.

As this thought fills the heart, the faith of the indwelling though hidden presence will influence; the Holy Place will be ruled from the Most Holy. The world of consciousness in the soul, with all its thoughts and feelings, its affections and purposes, will come and surrender themselves to the Holy Power that sits within on the throne. Amid the terrible experience of failure and sin a new hope will dawn. Though long I most earnestly strove, I could not keep the Holy Place for God, because I knew not that He kept the Most Holy for Himself. If I give Him there the glory due to His name, in the holy worship of the inner temple, He will send forth His light and His truth through my whole being,and through mind and will reveal His power to sanctify and to bless. And through the soul, thus coming ever more mightily under His rule, His power will work out even into the body. With passions and appetites within, yea, with every thought brought into subjection, the hidden Holy Spirit will through the soul penetrate ever deeper into the body. Through the Spirit the deeds of the body will be made dead, and the river of water, that flows from under 'the throne of God and the Lamb, will go through all the outer nature, with its cleansing and quickening power.

O Brother, do believe that you are the temple of the living God, and that the Spirit of God dwelleth in you ! You have been sealed with the Holy Spirit; He is the mark, the living assurance of your sonship and your Father's love. If this have hitherto been a thought that has brought you but little comfort, see if the reason is not here. You sought for Him in the Holy Place, amid the powers and services of your inner life which come within your vision, And you could hardly discern Him there. And so you could not appropriate the comfort and strength the Comforter was meant to bring. No, my brother, not there, not there. Deeper down, in the secret place of the Most High, there you will find Him. Within you! in your inmost part! there faith will find Him. And as faith worships in holy reverence before the Father, and the heart trembles at the thought of what it has found, wait in holy stillness on God to grant you the mighty working of His Spirit; wait in holy stillness for the Spirit, and be assured He will, as God, arise and fill His temple with His glory.

And then remember, the veil was but for a time. When the preparation was complete, the veil of the flesh was rent. As you yield your soul's inner life to the inmost life of the Spirit, as the traffic between the Most Holy and the Holy becomes more true and unbroken, the fullness of the time will come in your soul. In the power of Him, in whom the veil was rent that the Spirit might stream forth from His glorified body, there will come to you, too, an experience in which the veil shall be taken away, and the Most Holy and the Holy be thrown into one. The hidden glory of the Secret Place will stream into your conscious daily life: the service of the Holy Place will all be in the power of the Eternal Spirit.

Brother, let us fall down and worship! 'Be silent, all flesh, before the Lord; for he is waked up out of His holy habitation.'

Most Holy God! in adoring wonder I bow before Thee in presence of this wondrous mystery of grace: my spirit, soul, and body Thy temple. In deep silence and worship I accept the blessed revelation, that in me too there is a Holiest of all, and that there Thy hidden Glory has its abode. O my God, forgive me that I have so little known it. I do now tremblingly accept the blessed truth: God the Spirit, the Holy Spirit, who is God Almighty, dwells in me. O my Father, reveal within what it means, lest I sin against Thee by saying it and not living it.

Blessed Jesus! to Thee, who sittest upon the throne, I yield my whole being. In Thee I trust to rise up in power and have dominion within me. In Thee I believe for the full 'Streaming forth of the living waters. Blessed Spirit! Holy Teacher! Mighty Sanctifier! Thou art within me. On Thee do I wait all the day. I belong to Thee. Take entire possession of me for the Father and the Son Amen.

Chapter 25
The Ministry of the Spirit

'Our sufficiency is of God ; who also made us sufficient as ministers of a new covenant; not of the letter, but of the Spirit: for the letter killeth, but the Spirit giveth life. But if the ministration of death came with glory, how shall not rather the ministration of the Spirit be with glory ?' 2 Corinthians 3:6, 7.

In none of his Epistles does Paul expound his conception of the Christian ministry so clearly and fully as in the second to the Corinthians. The need of vindicating his apostleship against detractors, the consciousness of Divine Power and Glory working in him in the midst of weakness, the intense longing of his loving heart to communicate what he had to impart, stir his soul to its very depths, and he lays open to us the inmost secrets of the life that makes one a true minister of Christ and His Spirit. In our text we have the central thought: he finds his sufficiency of strength, the inspiration and rule of all his conduct, in the fact that he has been made a minister of the Spirit. If we take the different passages in which mention is made of the Holy Spirit in the first half of the Epistle,' we shall see what, in his view, the place and work of the Holy Spirit in the ministry is, and what the character of a ministry under His leading and in His power.

In the Epistle, Paul will have to speak with authority. He begins by placing himself on a level with his readers. In his first mention of the Spirit he tells them that the Spirit that is in him is no other than is in them. ' Now He which stablisheth us with you in Christ, and anointed us, is God; who also sealed us, and gave us the earnest of the Spirit in our hearts' (1:21, 22). The anointing of the believer with the Spirit, bringing him into fellowship with Christ, the anointed One, and revealing what He is to us; the sealing, marking him as God's own, and giving him assurance of it; the earnest of the Spirit, securing at once the foretaste and the fitness for the heavenly inheritance in glory: of all this he and they are together partakers. However much there was among the Corinthians ,that was wrong and unholy, Paul speaks to them, thinks of them, and loves them as one in Christ 'He that stablisheth us with you in Christ, and anointed us,'-this deep sense of unity fills his soul, comes out throughout the Epistle, and is the secret of his power. See 1: 6, 10, 2: 3 : 'My joy is the joy of you all;' 4:5 : 'ourselves your servants ;' 4: 10-12 : ' death worketh in us, life in you;' 4:15 : 'all things are for your sakes;' 6:11, 7: 3 : 'you are in our hearts to live and die with you.' If the unity of the Spirit, the consciousness of being members one of another, be necessary in all believers, how much more must it be the mark of those who are ministers? The power of the ministry to the saints depends upon the unity of the Spirit; the full recognition of believers as partakers of the anointing. But to this end the minister must himself live as an anointed and sealed one, making manifest that he has the earnest of the Spirit in his heart.

The second passage is 3: 3: 'Ye are an epistle of Christ, ministered by us, written with the Spirit of the living God; not in tables of stone, but in tables that are hearts of flesh.' As distinct an act of God as was the writing of the law on the tables of stone, is the writing of the law of the Spirit in the new covenant, and of the name of Christ on the heart. It is a divine work, in which, as truly as God wrote of old, the Holy Spirit uses the tongue of His minister as His pen. It is this truth that needs to be restored in the ministry: not only that the Holy Spirit is needed, but that He waits to do the work, and that He will do it, when the right relation to Him is maintained. Paul's own experience at Corinth (Acts 18: 5-11 ; 1 Cor. 2:3) teaches us what conscious weakness, what fear and trembling, what sense of absolute helplessness may be, or rather is, needed, if the power of God is to rest upon us. Our whole Epistle confirms this: it was as a man under sentence of death, bearing about the dying of the Lord Jesus, that the power of Christ wrought in him. The Spirit of God stands in contrast to the flesh, the world, and self, with its life and strength; it is as these are broken down, and the flesh has nothing to glory in, that the Spirit will work. Oh that every minister's tongue might be prepared for the Holy Spirit to use it as a pen wherewith He writes!

Then come the words of our text (3: 6, 7), to teach us what the special characteristic is of this New Covenant Ministry of the Spirit: it gives life.' The antithesis, 'the letter killeth,' applies not only to the law of the Old Testament, but, according to the teaching of Scripture, to all knowledge which is not in the quickening power of the Spirit. We cannot insist upon it too earnestly, that, even as the law, though we know it was 'spiritual,' so the gospel too has its letter. The gospel may 'be preached most clearly and faithfully; it may exert a strong moral influence ; and yet the faith that comes of it may stand in the wisdom of men, and not in the power of God. If there is one thing the Church needs to cry for on behalf of its ministers and students, it is that the Ministry of the Spirit may be restored in its full power. Pray that God may teach them what it is personally to live in the anointing, the scaling, the earnest of the Indwelling Spirit ; what it is to know that the letter killeth ; what it is that the Spirit in very deed giveth life; and what, above all, the personal life is under which the Ministry of the Spirit can freely work.

Paul now proceeds to contrast the two dispensations and the different characters of those who live in them.' He points out how, as long as the mind is blinded, there is a veil on the heart which can only be taken away as we turn to the Lord. And then he adds (3:17, 18): 'Now the Lord is the Spirit ; and where the Spirit of the Lord is, there is liberty. But we all, with unveiled face beholding as in a mirror the glory of the Lord, are transformed into the same image, from glory to glory, even as from the Lord the Spirit.' It is because God 'is a Spirit' that He can give the Spirit. It was when our Lord Jesus was exalted into the life of the Spirit that He became 'the Lord the Spirit,' could give the New Testament Spirit, and in the Spirit come Himself to His people. The disciples knew Jesus long, without knowing Him as the Lord the Spirit. Paul speaks of this, too, with regard to himself (2 Cor.5:16). There may in the ministry be much earnest gospel preaching of the Lord Jesus as the Crucified One, without the preaching of Him as the Lord the Spirit. It is only as the latter truth is apprehended, and experienced, and then preached, that the double blessing will come that Paul speaks of here. 'Where the Spirit of the Lord is, is liberty:' believers will be led into the glorious liberty of the children of God (Rom.8: 2 ; Gal. 5:1,18). And then: 'we are transformed into the same image, even as from the Lord the Spirit:' He will do the work for which He was sent-to reveal the glory of the Lord in us and as we behold that glory, we shall be changed from glory to glory. Of the time before Pentecost it was written: 'The Spirit was not yet, because Jesus was not yet glorified.' But when He had been 'justified in the Spirit, and received up in glory,' the Spirit came forth from 'the excellent glory' into our hearts, that we, with unveiled face beholding the glory of the Lord might be changed into His likeness, from glory to glory. What a calling ! the Ministry of the Spirit! to hold up the glory of the Lord to His redeemed, and to be used by His Spirit in working their transformation into His likeness. 'Therefore, seeing we have this ministry, we faint not.' It is as the knowledge and acknowledgment of Christ as the Lord the Spirit, and of the Spirit, of Christ as changing believers into His likeness, lives in the Church, that the ministry among believers will be in Life and Power,-in very deed, a Ministry of the Spirit.

The power of the ministry on the Divine side is the Spirit; on the human, it is here, as everywhere, faith. The next mention of the Spirit is in 4:13 : ' Having the same Spirit of faith,' After having, in chap.3, set forth the glory of the Ministry of the Spirit, and, 4:1-6, the glory of the Gospel it preached, he turns to the vessels in which this treasure is. He has to vindicate his apparent weakness. But he does far more. Instead of apologizing for it, he expounds its Divine meaning and glory, He proves how just this constituted his power, because in his weakness Divine power could work. It has been so ordained, 'that the excellency of the power may be of God, and not of us.' So his perfect fellowship with Jesus was maintained as he bore about 'the putting to death of the Lord Jesus, that the life of Jesus also might be manifested in his mortal body.' So there was even in his sufferings something of the vicarious element that marked his Lord's: 'So then death worketh in us, but life in you.' And then he adds, as the expression of the animating power that sustained him through all endurance and labour: 'But having the same Spirit of faith,' of which we read in the, Scripture, 'according to that which is written, I believed, and therefore did I speak; we also believe, and therefore we also speak; knowing that He which raised up the Lord Jesus shall raise up us also with Jesus, and shall present us with you.'

Faith is the evidence of things not seen. It sees the Invisible, and lives in it. Beginning with trust in Jesus, ' in whom, though ye see Him not, yet believing, ye rejoice,' it goes on through the whole of the Christian life. Whatever is of the Spirit, is by faith. The great work of God, in opening the heart of His child to receive more of the Spirit, is to school his faith into more perfect freedom from all that is seen, and the more entire repose in God, even to the assurance that God dwelleth and worketh mightily in his weakness. For this end trials and sufferings are sent. Paul uses very remarkable language in regard to his sufferings in the first chapter (ver. 9): 'We ourselves have had the sentence of death in ourselves, that we should not trust in ourselves, but in God which raiseth the dead.' Even Paul was in danger of trusting in himself. Nothing is more natural; all life is confident of self; and nature is consistent with itself till it dies. For the mighty work he had to do, he needed a trust in none less than the Living God, who raiseth the dead. To this God led him by giving him, in the affliction which came upon him in Asia, the sentence of death in himself. The trial of his faith was its strength. In our context he returns to this thought: the fellowship of the dying of Jesus is to him the means and the assurance of the experience of the power of Christ's life. In the spirit of this faith he speaks: 'Knowing that He which raised up Jesus shall raise up us also.'

It was not until Jesus had died that the Spirit of life could break forth from Him. The life of Jesus was born out of the grave: it is a life out of death. It is as we daily die, and bear about the dying of Jesus; as flesh and self are kept crucified and mortified; as we have in ourselves God's sentence of death on all that is of self and nature,that the life and the Spirit of Jesus will be manifest in us. And this is the Spirit of faith, that in the midst of weakness and apparent death, it counts on God that raiseth the dead. And this is the Ministry of the

Spirit, when faith glories in infirmities, that the power of Christ may rest upon it. It is as our faith does not stagger at the earthiness and weakness of the vessel, as it consents that the excellency of the power shall be, not from ourselves, or in anything we feel, but of God alone, that the Spirit will work in the power of the living God.

We have the same thought in the two remaining passages. In chap. 5:5, he speaks again of 'the earnest of the Spirit' in connection with our groaning and being burdened. And then in chap.6: 6, the Spirit is introduced in the midst of the mention of his distresses and labors as the mark of his ministry. 'In everything commending ourselves, as the ministers of God, in much patience, in afflictions, . . . in the Holy Ghost, . . . as dying, and yet, behold, we live; as chastened, and not killed; as sorrowful, yet always rejoicing; as poor, yet making many rich.' The Power of Christ in the Holy Spirit was to Paul such a living reality, that the weakness of the flesh only led him the more to rejoice and to trust it. The Holy Spirit's dwelling and working in Him was consciously the secret spring and the Divine power of his ministry.

We may well ask, Does the Holy Spirit take the place in our ministry He did in Paul's ? There is not a minister or member of the Church who has not a vital interest in the answer. The question is not whether the doctrine of the absolute need of the Holy Spirit's working is admitted; but whether there is given to the securing of is presence and working that proportion of the time and life, of the thought and faith of the ministry, which His place, as the Spirit of the Lord Jesus on the Throne, demands. Has the Holy Spirit the place in the Church which our Lord Jesus would wish Him to have? When our hearts open to the inconceivably glorious Truth that He is the Mighty Power of God dwelling in us, that in Him the Living Christ works through us, that He is the Real Presence with us of the Glorified Lord on the Throne, we shall feel that the one need of the ministry and the Church is this: to wait at the footstool of the Throne without ceasing for the clothing with the Power that comes from on high. The Spirit of Christ, in His love and power, in His death and life, is the Spirit of the ministry. As it possesses this, it will be what the Head of the Church meant it to be, the Ministry of the Spirit.

Blessed Father! we thank Thee for the institution of the Ministry of the Word, as the great means through which our exalted Lord does His saving work by the Holy Spirit. We thank Thee that it is a Ministry of the Spirit, and for all the blessing Thou hast wrought through it in the world. Our prayer is, most Blessed God! that Thou wouldst increasingly and manifestly make it throughout Thy Church what Thou wouldst have it be-a Ministry of the Spirit and of Power.

Give Thy servants and people everywhere a deep sense of how much it still comes short of Thy purpose. Reveal how much there is in it of trust in the flesh, of man's zeal and strength, of the wisdom of this world. Teach all Thy true servants the holy secret of giving place to the Spirit of Christ, that He may use them. May the conscious presence of Christ in their hearts by the Holy Spirit give them great boldness of speech. May the power of the Holy Spirit in their whole life make them fit vessels for Him to use in teaching others. May Divine Power in the midst of weakness be the mark of their public ministry.

Teach Thy people to wait on their teaching, to receive it, to plead with Thee for it as a Ministry of the Spirit. And may the lives of believers increasingly be, in the power of such a ministry, those of men led and sanctified by the Holy Ghost. Amen,

' We are also weak In Him, but shall live with Him through the power of God toward you.' With martyrs and missionaries, persecution and tribulation have been the fellowship of Christ's suffering and weakness, His Power and Spirit. We may invite neither persecutions nor suffering ; how can in our days this fellowship of Christ's suffering and dying, the rending of the flesh, so indispensable to the Ministry of the Spirit, be maintained ? In a deep entering into the needs and the sorrows of the suffering humanity around us. And in that self-denial which in nothing allows the flesh, the self-life, to have its way, but increasingly seeks in utter weakness to make way for Christ's power to work, and depends upon His Spirit.

Chapter 26
The Spirit and the Flesh.

'Are you so foolish? having begun in the Spirit, are ye now perfected in the flesh?' Galatians 3:3

'We are the circumcision, who worship by the Spirit of God and glory in Christ Jesus, and have no confidence in the flesh; that I myself might have confidence even in the flesh.' Philippians 3:3

The flesh is the name by which Scripture designates our fallen nature, - soul and body. The soul at creation was placed between the spiritual or Divine and the sensible or worldly to each its due, and guide them into that union which would result in man attaining his destiny, a spiritual body. When the soul yielded to the temptation of the sensible, it broke away from the rule of the Spirit and came under the power of the body-it became flesh. And now the flesh is not only without the Spirit, but even hostile to it;`the flesh lusteth against the Spirit.'

In this antagonism of the flesh to the Spirit there are two sides. On the one hand, the flesh lusts against the Spirit in its committing sin and transgressing God's law. On the other hand, its hostility to the Spirit is no less manifested in its seeking to serve God and do His will. In yielding to the flesh, the soul sought itself instead of the God to whom the Spirit linked it; selfishly prevailed over God's will; selfishness became its ruling principle. And now, so subtle and mighty is his spirit of self, that the flesh, not only in sinning against God, but even when the soul learns to serve God, still asserts its power, refuses to let the Spirit alone lead, and, in its efforts to be religious ,is still the great enemy that ever hinders and quenches the Spirit. It is owing to this deceitfulness of the flesh that there often takes place what Paul speaks of to the Galatians:'Having begun in the Spirit, are ye now perfected in the flesh ? ' Unless the surrender to the Spirit be very entire, and the holy waiting on Him be kept up in great dependence and humility, what has been begun in the Spirit, very easily and very speedily passes over into confidence in the flesh. And the remarkable thing is, what at first sight might appear a paradox, that just where the flesh seeks to serve God, there it becomes the strength of sin.

Do we not know, how the Pharisees, with 'self-righteousness and carnal religion, fell into pride and selfishness, and became the servants of sin? Was it not just among the Galatians, of whom Paul asks the question about perfecting in flesh what was begun in the Spirit, and whom he has so to warn against the righteousness of works, that the works of the flesh were so manifest,and that they were in danger of devouring one another? Satan has no more crafty device for keeping souls in bondage than inciting them to a religion in the flesh. He knows that the power of flesh can never please God or conquer sin, and in due time the flesh that has gained supremacy over the Spirit in the service of God, will assert and maintain that same supremacy in the service of sin. It is only where the Spirit truly and unceasingly has the entire lead and rule in the life of worship, that it will have the power to lead and rule in the life of practical obedience. If I am to deny self in: intercourse with men, to conquer selfishness and temper and want of love, I must first learn to deny self in the intercourse with God. There the soul, seat of self, must learn to bow to the Spirit, where God dwells.

The contrast between the worship in the Spirit and the trusting in the flesh is very beautifully expressed in Paul's description of the true circumcision, -the circumcision of the heart,-whose praise is not of men, but of God: `Who worship the Spirit of God, and glory in Christ Jesus, and put no confidence in the flesh.' Placing the glorying in Christ Jesus in the center, as the very essence of the Christian faith and life, he marks on the one hand the great danger by which it is beset, on the other the safeguard by which its full enjoyment is secured. Confidence in the flesh is the one thing above all others that renders the glorying in Christ Jesus of none effect ; worship by the Spirit the one thing that alone can make it indeed life and truth. May the Spirit reveal to us what it is thus to glory in Christ Jesus!

That there is a glorying in Christ Jesus that is accompanied by much confidence in the flesh, all history and experience teach us. Among the Galatians it was so. The teachers whom Paul used so earnestly were all preachers of Christ His cross. But they preached it, not as men taught by the Spirit to know what the infinite and pervading influence of that cross must be, but those who; having had the beginnings of God's Spirit, had yet allowed their own wisdom and their thoughts to say what that cross meant, and so reconciled it with a religion which to a very extent was legal and carnal. And the story of the Galatian Church is repeated to this day even in the Churches that are most confidently assured that they are free from the Galatian error. Just notice how often the doctrine of justification faith is spoken of as if that were the only teaching of the Epistle, while the doctrine of the Spirit's indwelling as received by faith, and walking by the Spirit, is hardly mentioned.

Christ crucified is the wisdom of God. The confidence in the flesh, in connection with the glorying in Christ, is seen in confidence in its own wisdom. Scripture is studied, and preached, and heard, and believed in, very much in the power of the natural mind with little insistance upon the absolute need the Spirit's personal teaching. It is seen in the absolute confidence with which men know that they have the truth, though they have it far more from human than Divine teaching, and in the absence of that teachableness that waits for God to reveal His truth in His own light.

Christ, through the Holy Spirit, is not only the Wisdom but the Power of God. The confidence in the flesh, along with much glorying in Christ Jesus, to be seen and felt in so much of the work of the Christian Church in which human effort and human arrangement take a much larger place than the waiting on the Power that comes from on high. In the larger ecclesiastical organizations, in individual churches and circles, in the inner life of the heart and closet--alas! how much unsuccessful effort, what oft-repeated failure, is to be traced to this one evil! There is no want of acknowledging Christ, His person and work, as our only hope, no want of giving Him the glory, and yet so much confidence in the flesh, rendering it of none effect.

Let me here ask again, whether there be not many a one striving earnestly for a life in the fullness of consecration and the fullness of blessing who will find here the secret of failure. To help such has been one of my first objects and most earnest prayers in writing this book. As in sermon or address, in book or conversation or private prayer, the fullness of Jesus was opened up to them, with the possibility of a holy life in Him, the soul felt it all so beautiful and so simple, that nothing could any longer keep it back. And perhaps, as it accepted of what was seen to be so sure and so near, it entered into an enjoyment and experienced a power before unknown. It had now learnt to glory in Christ Jesus! But it did not last. There was a worm at the root. Vain was the search for what the cause of the discomfiture was, or the way of restoration. Frequently the only answer that could be found was that the surrender was not entire, or faith's acceptance not perfect. And yet the soul felt sure that it was ready, as far as it knew, to give up all, and it did long to let Jesus have all and to trust Him for all. It could almost become hopeless of an impossible perfection, if perfect consecration and perfect faith were to be the condition of the blessing. And the promise had been that it would all be so simple,--just the life for the poor and feeble ones.

Listen, my brother, to the blessed teaching of God's word today. It was the confidence in the flesh that spoilt thy glorying in Christ Jesus. It was Self doing what the Spirit alone can do;it was Soul taking the lead, in the hope that the

Spirit would second its efforts, instead of trusting the Holy Spirit to lead and do all, and then waiting Him. It was following Jesus, without the denial of self. It was this was the secret trouble. Come and listen to Paul as he tells of the only safeguard against this danger: ' We are the circumcision, who worship by the Spirit of God, and glory in Christ Jesus, and have no confidence in the flesh.' Here are the two elements of spiritual worship, The Spirit exalts Jesus, and abases the flesh. And if we would truly glory in Jesus, and have Him glorified in us, if we would know the glory of Jesus in personal and unchanging experience, free from the impotence which always marks the efforts of the flesh, we must simply learn what this worship of God by the Spirit is.

I can only repeat, once again, what it is the purpose of this whole book to set forth as God's truth from His blessed word: Glory in Christ Jesus. Glory in Him as the Glorified One who baptizeth with the Holy Spirit. In great simplicity and trustfulness believe in Him as having given His own Spirit within you. Believe in that gift; believe in the Holy Spirit dwelling within you. Accept this the secret of the life of Christ in you: the Holy Spirit is dwelling in the hidden recesses of your Spirit. Meditate on it, believe Jesus and His Word concerning it, until your soul bows with holy fear and awe before God under the glory of the truth: the Holy Spirit of God is indeed dwelling in me.

Yield yourself to His leading. We have seen that leading is not first in the mind or thoughts, but in the life and disposition. Yield yourself to God, to be guided by the Holy Spirit in all your conduct. He is promised to those who love Jesus and obey Him: fear not to say that He knows you love and do obey Him with your whole heart. Remember, then, what the one central object of His coming was : to restore the departed Lord Jesus to His disciples. `I will not leave you orphans,' said Jesus ; ' I will come again to you.' I cannot glory a distant Jesus, from whom I am separated. When I try to do it, it is a thing of effort; I must have the help of the flesh to do it. I can only truly glory in a present Saviour, whom the Holy Spirit glorifies, reveals in His glory, within me. As He does this, the flesh is abased, and kept in its place of crucifixion as an accursed thing: as He does it, the deeds of the flesh are made to die. And my sole religion will be: no confidence in the flesh, glorying in Christ Jesus, worship by the Spirit of God.

Beloved believer! having begun in the Spirit, continue, go on, persevere in the Spirit. Beware of for one single moment, continuing or perfecting a work of the Spirit in the flesh. Let 'no confidence in the flesh' be your battle-cry ; let, a deep trust of the flesh and fear of grieving the Spirit by walking after the flesh, keep you very low and humble before God. Pray God for the spirit of revelation,that you may see how Jesus is all and does all, and how by the Holy Spirit a Divine

Life indeed takes the place of your life, and Jesus is enthroned as the Keeper and Guide and Life of the soul.

Blessed God and Father! We thank Thee for the wondrous provision Thou hast made for Thy children's drawing nigh to Thee, glorying in Christ Jesus, and worshipping by the Spirit. Grant, we pray Thee, that such may be our life and all our religious service.

We feel the need of asking Thee to show us how the one great hindrance to such a life is the power of the flesh and the efforts of, the self-life. Open our eyes, we pray Thee, to this snare of Satan. May we all see how secret and how subtle is the temptation to have confidence in the flesh, and how easily we are led to, perfect , in the flesh what has been begun in the Spirit. May we learn to trust Thee to work in us by Thy Holy Spirit, both to will and to do.

Teach us, too, we pray Thee, to know how the flesh can be conquered and its power broken. In the death of Thy beloved Son our old man has been crucified: may we count all things but loss to be made conformable to that death, and have the old nature kept in the place of death. We do yield ourselves to the lead and rule of Thy Holy Spirit. We do believe that through the Spirit Christ is our life, so that instead of the life of effort and work, an entirely new life works within us. Our Father—in faith we give up all to Thy Spirit to be our life in us. Amen.

Chapter 27
The Spirit through Faith.

'Christ hath redeemed us from the curse, that upon the Gentiles might come the blessing of Abraham in Christ Jesus ; we might receive the promise of the Spirit through faith.' Galatians 3:13,14.

The word faith is used the first time in Scripture in connection with Abraham. His highest praise, the secret of his strength for obedience, and what made him so pleasing to God, that he believed God; and so he became the Father of all them that believe, and the great example of the blessing which the Divine favor sows, and the path in which it comes. Just as God proved Himself to Abraham the God who quickens the dead, He does to us too, in fuller measure, in giving us the Spirit of His own Divine to dwell in us. And just as this quickening power came to Abraham through faith, so the blessing of Abraham, as now made manifest in Christ, even the promise of the Spirit, is made ours by faith. All the lessons of Abraham's life center in this: ` We receive the promise of the Spirit through faith.' If we want to know what the Faith is through which the Spirit is received, how that faith comes and grows, we must study what God has taught us of it in Abraham's story.

In Abraham's life we see what faith is: the spiritual sense by which man recognizes and accepts the revelation of his God, a spiritual sense called forth and awakened by that revelation. It was because God had chosen Abraham, and determined to reveal Himself, that Abraham became a man of faith. Each new revelation was an act of the Divine Will; it is the Divine Will, and the revelation in which it carries out its purpose, that is the cause and the life of faith. The more distinct the revelation or contact with God, the deeper is faith stirred in the soul. Paul speaks of 'trust in the Living God:' it is only as the Living One, in the quickening power of the Divine Life, draws nigh and touches the soul, that living faith will be called forth. Faith is not an independent act, by which in our own strength we take what God says. Nor is it an entirely passive state, in which we only suffer God to do to us what He will. But it is that receptivity of soul in which, as God comes near, and as His living Power speaks to us and touches us, we yield ourselves and accept His word and His working.

It is thus very evident that faith has two things to deal with: first the Presence, and then the Word of the Lord. It is only the Living Presence that makes the Living Word; so the Kingdom comes not in word only, but in power. It is on this account that there is so much reading and preaching of the word that bears so little fruit; so much straining and praying for faith, with so little result. Men deal with the word more than with the Living God. Faith has very truly been defined as `Taking God at His word.' With many this has only meant, taking the word as God's; they did not see the force of the thought, Taking God at His word. A key or a door handle has no value until I use it for the lock and the door I want to open; it is alone in direct and living contact with God Himself that the word can work effectually and open the heart for God. Faith takes God at His word; it can only do this when and as He gives Himself. I may have in God's book all His precious promises most clear and full; I may have learnt perfectly to understand how I have but to trust the promise to have it fulfilled; and yet utterly fail to find the longed for blessing. The Faith that enters on the inheritance is the attitude of soul which waits for God Himself, first to speak His word to me, and then to do the thing which He hath spoken. Faith is fellowship with God; faith is surrender to God; the impression made by His drawing nigh, the possession He takes of the soul by His word, holding and preparing it for His work. When once it has been awakened, it watches for every appearing of the Divine Will; it listens for and accepts ever indication of the Divine Presence; it looks for and expects the fulfillment of every Divine Promise.

Such was the faith through which Abraham inherited the promises. Such is the faith by which the blessing of Abraham comes upon the Gentiles in Christ Jesus, and by which we thus receive the promise of the Spirit. In all our study of the work of the Holy Spirit, and of the way in which He comes, from His first sealing us, to His full indwelling and streaming forth, let us hold fast this word: ' We receive the promise of the Spirit through faith.' Whether the believer be striving for the full consciousness that the Spirit dwells within, for a deeper assurance of His shedding abroad of God's love in the heart, for a larger growth of all His fruits, for the clearer experience of His guiding into all truth, or for the induement of power to labor and to bless, let him remember that the law of faith, on which the whole economy of grace is grounded, here demands its fullest application: ` According to your faith be it unto you.' ` We receive the promise of the Spirit through faith.' Let us seek for Abraham's blessing in Abraham's faith.

Let, in this matter, our faith begin where his began: in meeting God and waiting on God. 'The Lord appeared unto Abraham . . . . And Abraham fell on his face: and God talked with him: Let us look up to our God and Father as the

Living God, who Himself, by His Omnipotent Quickening Power,to do this wonderful thing for us : to fill us with His Holy Spirit. The blessing He has for us is the same He gave to Abraham, but only larger, fuller, and more wonderful. To Abraham, both when his own was now as dead, and later on, when his son already bound on the altar, the prey of death, He came as the Life - giving God. ` He believed who quickeneth the dead.' ` He offered up Isaac accounting God able to raise him up.' To us He comes, offering to fill spirit, soul, and body the power of a Divine life, through the Holy Spirit dwelling in us. Let us be like Abraham. Looking at the promise of God, he wavered not through unbelief, but waxed strong through faith, giving glory to God, and being fully assured that what He had promised, He was able also to perform.' Let us have our souls filled with the faith of Him who has promised, our hearts fixed on Him who is able to perform : it is faith in God opens the heart for God, and prepares to submit to and receive His Divine working. God waits on us to fill us with His Spirit: oh, let us wait on Him. God must do it all with a Divine doing, most mightily and most blessed: let us wait on Him. To read and think, to long and pray, to consecrate ourselves and grasp the promise, to hold fast the blessed truth that the Spirit dwells within us; all this is good in its place, but does not, bring the blessing. The one thing needful is, to have the heart filled with faith in the Living God; in that faith to abide in living contact with Him, in that faith to wait, and worship, and work, as in His Holy Presence. In such fellowship with God, the Holy Spirit fills the heart.

When we have taken up this position, let us keep in it ; we are then in the right state for the Spirit, in such measure as He already has had access to us, further revealing what God has prepared for us.' As we then think of some special manifestation of the Spirit, of which the conviction of need has been wrought, or go to the promises of the word to be led into all the Will of God concerning the life of the Spirit in us, we shall be kept in that humbling sense of dependence out of which childlike trust is most surely begotten. We shall be preserved from that life of strain and effort which has so often led to failure, because in the very attempt to serve God in the Spirit we were having or seeking confidence in the flesh, in something we felt, or did, or wished to do. The deep undertone of our life, in listening to God's word, or in asking God to listen to us, in silent meditation or public worship, in work for God or daily business, will be the assurance that overpowers every other certainty: `How much more will the Heavenly Father give,' has He given, and will He always be giving, `the Holy Spirit to them that ask Him.'

Such a faith will not be without its trials. Isaac, the God-given, faith-accepted life of Isaac, had to be given up to death, that it might be received back in resurrection-type, as life from the dead. The God-given experience of the Spirit's working many a time passes away, and leaves the soul apparently dull and dead. This is only until double lesson has been fully learnt; that a faith can rejoice in a Living God, even when all feeling and experience appear to contradict the promise ; and that the Divine life only enters as the life of the flesh is given to the death. The life of Christ is revealed as His death works in us, and as in weakness and nothingness we look to Him. We receive the promise of the Spirit through faith. As faith grows larger and broader, the receiving of promised Spirit will be fuller and deeper. Each new revelation of God to Abraham made his faith stronger and his acquaintance with God more intimate. When his God drew near, he knew what to expect; he knew to trust Him even in the most unlikely appearances, when asking the death of his son. It is the faith that waits every day on the Living God to reveal Himself ; the faith that in increasing tenderness of ear and readiness of service yields fully to Him and His Presence; the faith that knows that only as He wills to reveal Himself can the blessing come, but that because He always does love to reveal Himself, it will surely come;-- this faith receives the promise of the Spirit.

It was in God's Presence that this faith was wakened and strengthened in Abraham and the saints of old. It was in Jesus' Presence on earth that unbelief was cast out, and that little faith became strong. It was in the Presence of the glorified One that faith received the blessing of Pentecost. The Throne of God is now opened to us in Christ; it is become the Throne of God and the Lamb: as we tarry in humble worship, and walk in loving service before the Throne, the river of the water of life that flows from under it will flow into us, and through us, and out of us. `He that believeth, rivers of water shall flow out of him.'

Ever-blessed God! who dost in Thy Divine Love and Power reveal Thyself to each of Thy children as far as he can possibly bear it, increase within us, we pray Thee, the faith through which alone we can know or receive Thee. Whether Thou comest as the Almighty, or the Redeeming, or the Indwelling God, it is ever faith Thou seekest, and according to faith we receive. O Father! convince us deeply that we have just as much of the Spirit as we have faith.

Our Holy God! we know that it is Thy Presence wakens and works the faith in the soul that yields to Thee. Draw us mightily, we pray Thee, yea, resistibly into Thy Holy Presence, and keep us waiting there. Oh, deliver us from the terrible fascination of world and flesh, that Thy Divine Glory may be our all-absorbing desire, and our whole heart emptied to receive the Holy Spirit's revelation of Christ within. We desire to take Thy words, and let them dwell richly in us. We desire in stillness of soul to be silent unto God and wait for Him; to trust and believe that the Father hast given us His Spirit within us, and is in secret working to reveal His Son. O God! we do live the life of faith ; we do believe in the Holy Spirit. Amen.

Chapter 28
Walking by the Spirit.

Walk by the Spirit and ye shall not fulfill the lust of the flesh. They that are of Christ Jesus have crucified the flesh, with the passions and lusts thereof. If we live by the Spirit, by the Spirit let us also walk.' Galatians 5:16, 24, 25,

'If we live by the Spirit, by the Spirit let us walk.' These words suggest to us very clearly the -difference, between the sickly and the healthy Christian life. In the former the Christian is content to 'live by the Spirit;' he is satisfied with knowing that he has the new life; but be does not' walk by the Spirit.' The true believer, on the contrary, is not content without having his whole walk and conversation in the power of the Spirit. He walks by the Spirit, and so does not fulfill the lusts of the flesh.

As the Christian strives thus to walk worthy of God and well-pleasing to Him in all things, he is often sorely troubled at the power of sin, and asks what the cause may be that he so often fails in conquering it. The answer to this question he ordinarily finds in his want of faith or faithfulness, in his natural feebleness or the mighty power of Satan. Alas! if he rests content with this solution. It is well for him if he press on to find the deeper reason why all these things, from which Christ secured deliverance for him, still can overcome. One of the deepest secrets of the Christian life is the knowledge that the one great power that keeps the Spirit of God from ruling, that the last enemy that must yield to Him, is the flesh. He that knows what the flesh is, how it works and how it must be dealt with, will be conqueror.

We know how it was on account of their ignorance of this that the Galatians so sadly failed. It was this led them to attempt to perfect in the flesh what was begun in the Spirit (3: 3). It was this made them a prey to those who desired 'to make a fair show in the flesh' that they might 'glory in the flesh' (6:12, 13). They knew not how incorrigibly corrupt the flesh was. They knew not that, as sinful as our nature is when fulfilling its own lusts, as sinful is it when making 'a fair show in the flesh;' it apparently yields itself to the service of God, and undertakes to perfect what the Spirit had begun. Because they knew not this, they were unable to check the flesh in its passions and lusts; these obtained the victory over them, so that they did what they did not wish. They knew not that, as long as the flesh, self-effort, and self-will had any influence in serving God, it would remain strong to serve sin, and that the only way to render it impotent to do evil was to render it impotent in its attempts to do good.

It is to discover the truth of God concerning the flesh, both in its service of God and of sin, that this Epistle was written. Paul wants to teach then how the Spirit,--and the Spirit alone, is the power of the Christian life, and how this cannot be except as the flesh, with all that it means, is utterly and entirely set aside. And in answer to the question how this can be, he gives the wonderful answer which is one of the central thoughts of God's revelation. The crucifixion and death of Christ is the revelation not only of an atonement for sin, but of a power which frees from the actual dominion of sin, as it is rooted in the flesh. When Paul in the midst of his teaching about the walk in the Spirit (16-26) tells us, 'They that are Christ's have crucified the flesh with its passions and lusts,' he tells us what the only way is in which deliverance from the flesh is to be found. To understand this word, 'crucified. the flesh,' and abide in it, is the secret of walking not after the flesh but after the Spirit. Let each one who longs to walk by the Spirit try to enter into its meaning.

' The flesh'---in Scripture this expression means the whole of our human nature in its present condition under the power of sin. It includes our whole being, spirit, soul, and body. After the fall, God said, 'man is flesh' (Gen.6:3). All his powers, intellect, emotions, will,--all are under the power of the flesh. Scripture speaks of the will of the flesh of the mind of the flesh (fleshly mind), of the passions and lusts of the flesh. It tells us that in our flesh dwelleth no good: the mind of the flesh is at enmity against God. On this ground it teaches that nothing that is of the flesh, that the fleshly mind or will thinks or does, however fair the show it makes, and however much men may glory in it, can have any value in the sight of God. It warns us that our greatest danger in religion, the cause of our feebleness and failure, is our having confidence in the flesh, its wisdom and its work. It tells us that, to be pleasing to God, this flesh, with its self-will and self-effort, must entirely be dispossessed, to make way for the willing and the working of Another, even the Spirit of God. And that the only way to be made free from the power of the flesh, and have it put out of -the way, is to have it crucified and given over to the death.

'They that are of Christ Jesus have crucified the flesh.' Men often speak of crucifying the flesh as a thing that has to be done. Scripture always speaks of it as a thing that has been done, an accomplished fact. 'Knowing, this, that our old man was crucified with Him.' 'I have been crucified with Christ.' ' They that are of Christ Jesus have crucified the flesh.' ' The cross of our Lord Jesus Christ, through which the world hath been crucified unto me, and I unto the world.' What Christ, through the Eternal Spirit, did on the cross, He did not as an individual, but in the name of that human nature which, as its Head, He had taken upon Himself. Every one who accepts of Christ receives Him as the Crucified One, receives not only the merit, but the power of His crucifixion, is united and identified with Him, and is called on intelligently and voluntarily to realize and maintain that identification. ' They that are of Christ Jesus' have, in virtue of their accepting the crucified Christ as their life, given up their flesh to that cross which is of the very essence of the person and character of Christ as He now lives in heaven; they ' have crucified the flesh with its passions and lusts.'

But what does this mean: 'They have crucified the flesh'? Some are content with the general truth: the cross takes away the curse which there was on the flesh. Others think of causing the flesh pain and suffering, of the duty of denying and mortifying it. Others, again, of the moral influence the thought of the cross will exercise. In each of these views there is an element of truth. But if they are to be realized in power, we must go to the root-thought: to crucify the flesh is, to give it over to the curse. The Cross and the Curse are inseparable (Deut.21: 2 3 ; Gal.3:13). To say, ' Our old man has been crucified with Him,' ' I have been crucified with Christ,, means something very solemn and awful. It means this: I have seen that my old nature,myself, deserves the curse; that there is no way of getting rid of it but by death: I voluntarily give it to the death. I have accepted as my life the Christ who came to give Himself, His flesh, to the cursed death of the cross; who received His new life alone owing to that death and in virtue of it: I give my old man, my flesh, self, with its will and work, as a sinful, accursed thing, to the cross. It is nailed there: in Christ I am dead to it, and free from it. It is not yet dead ; but day by day in union with Christ will I keep it there, making dead, as they still seek to rise up, every one of its members and deeds in the power of the Holy Spirit.

The power of this truth depends upon its being known, accepted, and acted on. If I only know the cross in its Substitution, but not, as Paul gloried in it, in its Fellowship (Gal. 6:14), never can experience its power to sanctify. As the blessed truth of its Fellowship dawns upon me, I see how by faith I enter into and live in spiritual communion with that Jesus who, as my Head and Leader, made and proved the cross the only ladder to the Throne. This spiritual union, maintained by faith, becomes a moral one. I have the same mind or disposition that was in Christ Jesus. I regard the flesh as sinful, and only fit for the curse. I accept the cross, with its death to what is flesh, secured to me in Jesus, as the only way to become free from the power of self, and to walk in the new life by the Spirit of Christ.

The way in which this faith in the power of the cross acts, as at once the revelation and the removal of the curse and the power of the flesh, is very simple, and yet very solemn. I begin to understand that my one danger in living by the Spirit is yielding to the flesh or self in its attempt to serve God. I see that it renders the cross of Christ of none effect. (1 Cor.1:17 ; Gal.3:3, 5:12, 13 ; Phil. 3: 3, 4 ; Col.2:18-23.) 1 see how all that was of man and nature, of law and human effort, was for ever judged of God on Calvary. There flesh proved that, with all its wisdom and all its religion, it hated and rejected the Son of God. There God proved how the only way to deliver from the flesh was to give it to death as an accursed thing. I begin to understand that the one thing I need is: to look upon the flesh as God does; to accept of the death warrant the cross brings to everything in me that is of the flesh; to look upon it, and all that comes from it, as an accursed thing. As this habit of soul grows on me, I learn to fear nothing so much as myself. I tremble at the thought of allowing the flesh, my natural mind and will, to usurp the place of the Holy Spirit. My whole posture towards Christ is that of lowly fear, in the consciousness of having within me that accursed thing that is ever ready, as an angel of light, to intrude itself in the Holiest of all, and lead me astray to serve God, not in the Spirit of Christ, but in the power that is of nature. It is in,, such a lowly fear that the believer is taught to believe fully the need, but also the provision, of the Holy Spirit to take entirely the place which the flesh once had, and day by day to glory in the cross, of which he can say, 'By it I have been crucified to the world.'

We often seek for the cause of failure in the Christian life. We often think that because we are sound on what the Galatians did not understand,-justification by faith alone,their danger was not ours. Oh that we knew to what an extent we have allowed the flesh to work in our religion! Let us pray God for grace to know it as our bitterest enemy, and the enemy of Christ. Free grace does not only mean the pardon of sin ; it means the power of the New Life through the Holy Spirit. Let us consent to what God says of the flesh, and all that comes of it: that it is sinful, condemned, accursed. Let us fear nothing so much as the secret workings of our flesh. Let us accept the teaching of God's word: 'In my flesh dwelleth no good thing;' 'The carnal mind is enmity against God.' Let us ask God to show us how entirely the Spirit must possess us, if we are to be pleasing to Him in all things. Let us believe that as we daily glory in the cross, and, in prayer and obedience, yield the flesh to the death on the cross, Christ will accept our surrender, and will, by His Divine Power, maintain mightily in us the Life of the Spirit. And we shall learn not only to live by the Spirit, but, as those who are made free from the power of the flesh, by its crucifixion, maintained by faith, in very deed to walk by the Spirit.

Blessed God! I beseech Thee to reveal to me the full meaning of what Thy word has been teaching me, that it is as one who has crucified the flesh with its passions and lusts, that I can walk by the Spirit.

O my Father ! teach me to see that all that is of nature and of self is of the flesh ; that the flesh has been tested by Thee, and found wanting, worthy of nothing but the curse and death. Teach me that my Lord Jesus led the way, and acknowledged the justice of Thy curse, that I too might be willing and have the power to give it up to the cross as an accursed thing. Oh, give me grace day by day greatly to fear before Thee, lest I allow the flesh to intrude into the work of the Spirit, and to grieve Him. And teach me that the Holy Spirit has indeed been given to be the life of my life, and to fill my whole being with the power of the death and the life of my blessed Lord living in me.

Blessed Lord Jesus! who didst send Thy Holy Spirit, to secure the uninterrupted enjoyment of Thy Presence and Thy Saving Power within us, I yield myself to be entirely Thine, to live wholly and only under His leading. I do with my whole heart desire to regard the flesh as crucified and accursed. I solemnly consent to live as a crucified one. Savior! Thou dost accept my surrender; I trust in Thee to keep me this day walking through the Spirit. Amen.

Chapter 29
The Spirit of Love

The fruit of the Spirit is love.' Galatians 5:22.
I beseech you by the love of the Spirit.' Romans 15:30.
Who also declared unto us your love in the spirit, Colossians 1:8

Our subject today leads us up into the very center of the inner sanctuary. We are to think of the Love of the Spirit. We shall have to learn that love is not only one, among others, of the graces of the Spirit, is not only the chief among them, but that the Spirit is indeed nothing less than the Divine Love itself come down to dwell in us, and that we have only so much of the Spirit as we have of Love.

God is a Spirit: God Is Love. In these two words we have the only attempt that Scripture makes to give us, in human language, what may be called a definition of God.' As a Spirit, He has life in Himself, is independent of all around Him, and has power over all to enter into it, to penetrate it with His own life, to communicate Himself to it. It is through the Spirit that God is the Father of Christ, the Father of spirits, that He is the God of creation, that He is the God and Redeemer of man. All life is owing to the Spirit of God. And it is so because God is Love. Within Himself He is Love, as seen in the Father giving all He hath to the Son, and the Son seeking all He has in the Father. In this life of Love between the Father and the Son' the Spirit is the bond of fellowship. The Father is the Loving One, the Fountain; the Son the Beloved One, the great Reservoir of Love, ever receiving and ever giving back; the Spirit the Living Love that makes them one. In Him the Divine Life of Love hath its ceaseless flow and overflowing. It is that same love with which the -Father loves the Son that rests on us and seeks to fill us too, and it is through the Spirit that this Love of God is revealed and communicated to us. In Jesus it was the Spirit that led Him to the work of love for which He was anointed, to preach glad tidings to the poor and deliverance to the captives ; through that same Spirit He offered Himself a sacrifice for us. The Spirit comes to us freighted with all the love of God and of Jesus : the Spirit is the Love of God.

And when that Spirit enters us, His first work is: 'The love of God hath been shed abroad in our hearts by the Holy Ghost which was given unto us.' What He gives is not only the faith or the experience of how greatly God loves, but something infinitely more glorious. The Love of God, as a spiritual existence, as a Living Power, enters our hearts. It cannot be otherwise, for the Love of God exists in the Spirit; the outpouring of the Spirit is the in-pouring of Love. This Love now possesses the heart: that one same Love with which God loves Jesus, and ourselves, and all His children, and which overflows to all the world, is within us, and is, if we know it, and trust it, and give up to it, the power for us to live in too. The Spirit is the Life of the Love of God; the Spirit in us is the Love of God taking up abode within us.

Such is the relation between the Spirit and the Love of God; let us now consider the relation between our spirit and love. We must here again refer to what has been said of man's threefold nature, body, soul, and spirit, as constituted in creation and disorganized by the fall.' We saw how the soul, as the seat of self-consciousness, was to be subject to the spirit, the seat of the God consciousness. And how sin was simply self assertion, the soul refusing the rule of the spirit to gratify itself in the lust of the body. The fruit of that sin was that self ascended the throne of the soul, to rule there instead of God in the spirit. Selfishness thus became the ruling power in man's life. The self that had refused God His right at once refused fellow-man his due, and the terrible story of sin in the world is simply the history of the origin, the growth, the power, the reign of self. And it is only when the original order is restored when the soul gives the spirit the precedence it claims, and self is denied to make way for God, that selfishness will be conquered, and love toward our brother flow from love toward God. In other words, as the renewed spirit becomes the abode of the Spirit of God and His love, and as the regenerate man yields himself to let the Spirit have sole sway, that love will again become our life and our joy. To every disciple the Master says here again, 'Let him deny self and follow me.' Many a one has sought in vain to follow Jesus in His life of love, and could not, because he neglected what was so indispensable denying self. Self following Jesus always fails, because it cannot love as He loves.

If we understand this, we are prepared to admit the claim that Jesus makes, and that the world makes too, that our proof of discipleship is to be Love. The change we profess to have undergone is so Divine, the deliverance from the power of self and sin so complete, the indwelling of the Spirit of God's love is so real and true, and the provision made to enable us thus to live so sufficient, that love, or the new commandment, as the fulfilling of the law, ought to be the natural overflow of the new life in every believer. That it is not so is simply another proof of how little believers understand their calling to walk after the Spirit, really to be spiritual men. All the complaints that are continually being made by ourselves, or those around us, of tempers unconquered and of selfishness prevailing, of harsh judgments and unkind words, of the want of a Christlike meekness and patience and gentleness, of the little that is really being done by the majority of Christians in the way of self-sacrifice for the social and religious needs of the perishing around them,-all this is simply the proof that it has not yet been understood that to be a Christian just means to have the Spirit of Christ; just means to have His Love, to have been made by Him a fountain of Love springing up and flowing out in streams of living water. We know not what the Spirit is meant to be in us, because we have not accepted Him for what the Master gave. We are more carnal than spiritual.

It was thus with the Corinthians. In them we see the remarkable phenomenon of a Church, 'in everything enriched in Christ, in all utterance, and all knowledge, coming behind in no gift," abounding in everything in faith, and utterance, and knowledge,' and yet so sadly wanting in love. 'Whereas there is among you jealousy and strife, are ye not carnal?' The sad spectacle teaches us how, under the first movings of the Holy Spirit, the natural powers of the soul, knowledge, faith, utterance, may be mightily affected, without self yet being entirely surrendered ; and how thus many of the gifts of the Spirit may be seen, while the chief of all, Love, is sadly wanting. It teaches us how to be truly spiritual. It is not enough for the Spirit to take hold of these natural soul-endowments and rouse them to exercise in God's service. Something more is needed. He has entered the soul, that through it He may obtain a fixed and undivided sway in soul and spirit both, that with self deposed God may reign. And the token that self is deposed and that God does reign will be Love ; the surrender and the power to count nothing Life but Love, a life in the love of the Spirit.

Not very different was the state of the Galatians, to whom the words, 'The fruit of the Spirit is Love,' were addressed. Though their error was not that of the Corinthians, boasting of gifts and knowledge, but a seeking after and trusting in carnal observances and ordinances, the result was in both the same-the Spirit's full dominion was not accepted in the inner life of love, and so the flesh ruled in them, causing bitterness and envy and enmity. (Gal.5:15,16, 25, 26.) And even so it is still in much of what bears the name of the Christian Church. On the one hand the trust in gifts and knowledge, in soundness of creed and earnestness of work, on the other the satisfaction in forms and services, leaves the flesh in full vigour, not crucified with Christ, and so the Spirit is not free to work out true holiness or a life in the power of Christ's love. Oh, do let us learn the lesson, and pray God very fervently to teach it to His people, that a Church or a Christian professing to have the Holy Spirit must prove it in the first place by the exhibition of a Christlike love. Both in its gentleness in bearing wrong, and in its life of self-sacrifice to overcome the wrong, and to save all who are under its power, the life of Christ must be repeated in His members. The Spirit is indeed the Love of God come down to us.'

As searching and solemn as this truth is in this aspect, so comforting and encouraging is it in another. The Spirit is the Love of God come down to us. Then we have that love within our reach; it is indeed dwelling within us. Since the day when, in believing, we were sealed with the Holy Ghost, the love of God has been shed abroad in our hearts. 'The love of God hath been shed abroad in our hearts, through the Holy Ghost which was given unto us.' Though there may have been little to see of it in our lives, though we ourselves have hardly felt or known it, though the blessing has been unrecognized, there it was; with the Holy Spirit came down the Love of God into our hearts; the two could never be separated. And if we would now come to the experience of the blessing, we must just begin by a very simple faith in what the word says. The word is Spirit-breathed, the Divinely-prepared organ through which the Spirit reveals what He is and does. As we take that word as Divine Truth, the Spirit will make it Truth in us. Let us believe that the Holy Spirit, possessor and bearer to us of all God's Love, has been within our heart with all that Love ever since we became God's children. Because the veil of the flesh has never been rent in us, the outstreaming and power of that Love has been but feeble, and hidden from our consciousness. Let us believe that He dwells within us, to reveal as the Power of our Life, the Love of God in our hearts.

In this faith, that the Love-shedding Spirit is within us, let us look up to the Father in earnest prayer, to plead for His mighty working in our inner man, that Christ may dwell in our hearts, that we may be rooted and grounded in love, that our whole life may have its strength and nourishment in love. As the answer comes, the Spirit will first reveal to us the Love of God, the Love of the Father to Christ as His Love to us, the Love of Christ to us, the same with which the Father loved Him. Through the same Spirit this love then rises and returns to its Source, as our love to God and Christ. And because that Spirit has revealed that same love to all God's children around us, our experience of it as coming from God, or returning up to God, is ever one with love to the brethren. Just as the water descending in rain, and flowing out as fountains or streams, and rising up to heaven again as vapor, is all one, so the Love of God in its threefold form; His Love to us, our love to Him, and the love to each other as brethren. The Love of God is within thee by the Holy Spirit: believe it, and rejoice in it ; yield thyself to it as a Divine fire consuming the sacrifice and lifting it heavenward: exercise and practice it in intercourse with every one on earth. Then thou shalt understand

and prove that the Spirit of God is the Love of God.

Blessed Lord Jesus! in holy reverence I bow before Thee as Love Incarnate. The Father's love gave Thee. Thy coming was a mission of Love. Thy whole life was Love; Thy death its Divine seal. The one commandment Thou gavest Thy disciples was Love. Thy one prayer before the throne is that Thy disciples may be one, as Thou with the Father, and that His Love may be in them. The one chief trait of Thy likeness Thou longest to see in us is, that we love even as Thou lovest. The one irresistible proof to the world of Thy Divine mission will be the love of Thy disciples to each other. And the Spirit that comes from Thee to us is the very Spirit of Thy self-sacrificing love, teaching Thy saints to live and die for others, as Thou didst.

Holy Lord Jesus! look upon Thy Church, look upon our hearts. And wherever Thou seest that there is not love like Thine, oh, make haste and deliver Thy saints from all that is still selfish and unloving ' Teach them to yield that self, which cannot love, to the accursed cross, to await the fate it deserves. Teach us to believe that we can love, because the Holy Spirit hath been given us. Teach us to begin to love and serve, to sacrifice self and live for others, that love in action may learn its power, may be increased and perfected. Oh, teach us to believe that because Thou livest in us, Thy love is in us too, and we can love as Thou dost. Lord Jesus, Thou Love of God! Thine own Spirit is within us; oh, let Him break through, and fill our whole life with love. Amen.

Chapter 30
The Unity of the Spirit.

'That ye walk with all lowliness and meekness, with longsuffering, forbearing one another in love; giving diligence to keep the unity of the Spirit in the bond of peace. There is one body, and one Spirit.' Ephesians 4:1-4.

' Now there are diversities of gifts, but the same Spirit. . . . All these worketh one and the same Spirit, dividing to each one severally even as He will. For in one Spirit were we all baptized into one body; and were all made to drink of one Spirit.' 1 Corinthians 12: 4,11,13.

We know how, in the first three chapters of the Ephesians, Paul had set forth the glory of Christ Jesus as the Head of the Church, and the glory of God's grace in the Church as the Body of Christ, indwelt by the Holy Spirit, growing up into an habitation of God through the Spirit, and destined to be filled with all the fullness of God. Having thus lifted the believer to his true place in the heavenlies, with his life hid in Christ, he comes with him down to his life in the earthlies, and, in the second half of the Epistle, teaches how he is to walk worthy of his calling. And the very first lesson he has to give in regard to this life and walk on earth (Eph.4: 1-4) rests on the foundation-truth that the Holy Spirit has united him not only to Christ in heaven, but to Christ's body on earth. The Spirit dwells not only in Christ in heaven and in the believer on earth, but very specially in Christ's body, with all its members; and the full, healthy action of the Spirit can only be found where the right relation exists between the individual and the whole body, as far as he knows or comes into contact with it. His first care in his holy walk must be, therefore, to give diligence that the unity of the Spirit be maintained intact. Where this unity of the one Spirit and one body is fully acknowledged, the cardinal virtue of the Christian life will be lowliness and meekness (vers. 2, 3), in which each would forget and give up self for others; amid all differences and shortcomings, all would forbear one another in love. So the new commandment would be kept, and the Spirit of Christ, the Spirit of Love sacrificing itself wholly for others, would have free scope to do His blessed work.

The need of such teaching the first Epistle to the Corinthians remarkably illustrates. In that Church there were abundant operations of the workings of the Holy Spirit. The gifts of the Spirit were strikingly manifested, but the graces of the Spirit were remarkably absent. They understood not how there are diversities of gifts, but the same Spirit; how, amid all difference, one and the same Spirit divides to each severally as He will; how all had been baptized in one Spirit into one body, and all made to drink of one Spirit. They knew not the more excellent way, and that the chief of all the gifts of the Spirit is the Love that seeketh not its own, and only finds its life and its happiness in others.

To each believer who would fully yield himself to the leading of the Spirit, as well as to the Church as a whole, in its longings for the experience in power of all that the indwelling of the Spirit implies, the unity of the Spirit is a truth fraught with rich spiritual blessing. In previous writings I have more than once made use of the expression of Pastor Stockmaier: ' Have a deep reverence for the work of the Holy Spirit within thee.' That injunction needs as its complement a second one: Have a deep reverence for the work of the Holy Spirit in thy brother. This is no easy thing: even Christians, in other respects advanced, often fail here. The cause is not difficult to discover. In our books on education we are taught that the faculty of Discrimination, the observing of differences, is one of the earliest to be developed in children. The power of Combination, or the observing of the harmony that exists amid apparent diversity, is a higher one, and comes later; as the power of Classification, in its highest action, it is only found in true genius. The lesson finds most striking exemplification in the Christian life and Church. It needs but little grace to know where we differ from other Christians or churches, to contend for our views, or to judge their errors in doctrine or conduct. But this indeed is grace, where, amid conduct that tries or grieves us, or teaching that appears to us unscriptural or hurtful, we always give the unity of the Spirit the first place, and have faith in the power of love to maintain the living union amid outward separation.

Keep the unity of the Spirit : such is God's command to every believer. It is the New Commandment, to love one another, in a new shape, tracing the love to the Spirit in which it has its life. If you would obey the command, note carefully that it is the unity of the Spirit. There is a unity of creed or custom, of church or choice, in which the bond is more of the flesh than of the Spirit. Would you keep the unity of the Spirit, remember the following things.

Seek to know that in thyself in which the unity is to find its power of attachment and of victory. There is much in thee that is of self and of the flesh, and that can take part in a unity that is of this earth, but that will greatly hinder the unity of the Spirit. Confess that it is in no power or love of thine own that thou canst love; all that is of thyself is selfish, and reaches not to the true unity of the Spirit. Be very humble in the thought that it is only what is of God in thee that can ever unite with what appears displeasing to thyself. Be very joyful in the thought that there is indeed that in thee which can conquer self, and love even what seems unloving.

Study also to know and prize highly that in thy brother with which thou art to be united. As in thyself, so there is in him, but a little beginning, a hidden seed of the Divine life, surrounded by much that is yet carnal, and often is very trying and displeasing. It needs a heart very humble in the knowledge of how unworthy thou thyself art, and very loving in the readiness to excuse thy brother,for so did Jesus in the last night: 'the spirit indeed is willing, but the flesh is weak ' 'to look persistently at what there is in the brother of the image and Spirit of the Father. Estimate him not by what he is in himself, but by what he is in Christ, and as thou feelest how the same life and Spirit, which thou owest to free grace, is in him too, the unity of the Spirit will triumph over the difference and dislike of the flesh. The Spirit in thee, acknowledging and meeting the Spirit in thy brother, will bind thee in the unity of a life that is from above.

Keep this unity of the Spirit in the active exercise of fellowship. The bond between the members of my body is most living and real, maintained by the circulation of the blood and the life it carries. 'In one Spirit we were all baptized into one body! 'There is one body and one Spirit! The inner union of life must find expression and be strengthened in the manifested communion of love. Cultivate intercourse not only with those who are of one way of thinking and worshiping with thyself, lest the unity be more in the flesh than the Spirit. Study in all thy thoughts and judgments of other believers to exercise the love that thinketh no evil. Never say an unkind word of a child of God, as little as of others. Love every believer, not for the sake of what in him is in sympathy with thee or pleasing to thee, but for the sake of the Spirit of the Father which there is in him. Give thyself expressly and of set purpose to love and labor for God's children within thy reach, who through ignorance, or feebleness, or waywardness, know not that they have the Spirit, or are grieving Him. The work of the Spirit is to build up an habitation for God; yield thyself to the Spirit in thee to do the work. Recognize thy dependence upon the fellowship of the Spirit. in thy brother, and his dependence upon thee, and seek thy growth and his in the unity of love.

Take thy part in the united intercession that rises up to God for the unity of His Church. Take up and continue the intercession of the Great High Priest for all who believe, 'that they may be one.' The Church is one in the life of Christ and the love of the Spirit. It is, alas ! not one in the manifested unity of the

Spirit. Hence the need of the command: Keep the unity. Plead with God for the mighty workings of His Spirit in all lands and churches and circles of believers. When the tide is low, each little pool along the shore with its inhabitants is separated from the other by a rocky barrier. As the tide rises, the barriers are flooded over, and all meet in one great ocean. So it will be with the Church of Christ. As the Spirit of God comes, according to the promise, as floods upon the dry ground, each will know the power in himself and in others, and self disappear as the Spirit is known and honored.

And how is this wondrous change to be brought about, and the time hastened that the prayer be fulfilled, 'that they all may be one, that the world may know that Thou hast sent me, and hast loved them as Thou hast loved me ' ? Let each of us begin with himself. Resolve even now, beloved child of God, that this shall be the one mark of your life, the proof of your sonship, the having and knowing the Indwelling Spirit. If you are to unite, not with what pleases you, or is in harmony with your way of thinking and acting, but with what the Spirit in you sees and seeks in others, you must have given yourself entirely up to His way of thinking and acting. And if you are to do this, He must have the mastery of your whole being. You need to abide in the living and never ceasing consciousness that He dwelleth within you. You need to pray unceasingly that the Father may grant you, according to the riches of His glory, to be strengthened with might by His Spirit in the inner man. It is in the faith of the Triune God, the Father giving the Spirit in the name of the Son, and the Spirit dwelling within you; it is in this faith brought into adoring exercise at the footstool of God's throne ; it is in direct contact and fellowship with the Father and the Son, that the Spirit will take full possession, and pervade your entire being. The fuller His indwelling and the mightier His working is, the more truly spiritual your being becomes, the more will self sink away, and the Spirit of Christ use you in building up and binding together believers into an habitation of God, Christ's Spirit will be in you the holy anointing, the oil of consecration, to set you apart and fit you to be, as Christ was, a messenger of the Father's love. In the humility and gentleness of daily life, in the kindliness and forbearance of love amid all the differences and difficulties in the Church, in the warmhearted sympathy and self-sacrifice that goes out to find and help all who need help, the Spirit in you will prove that He belongs to all the members of the body as much as to you, and that through you His love reaches out to all around to teach and to bless.

Blessed Lord Jesus ! in Thy last night on earth Thy one prayer for Thy disciples was, 'Holy Father, keep them, that they may be one.' Thy one desire was to see them a united flock, all gathered and kept together in the One Almighty Hand of Love. Lord Jesus! now Thou art on the Throne, we come to

Thee with the same plea: Oh, keep us, that we may be one ! pray for us, Thou Great High Priest, that we may be made perfect in one, that the world may know that the Father hath loved us, as He loved Thee.

Blessed Lord! we thank Thee for the tokens that Thou art wakening in Thy Church the desire for the manifestation to the world of the unity of Thy people. Grant, we pray Thee, to this end the mighty workings of Thy Holy Spirit. May every believer know the Spirit that is in him, and that is in his brother, and in all lowliness and love keep the unity of the Spirit with those with whom he comes into contact. May all the leaders and guides of Thy Church be enlightened from above, that the unity of the Spirit may be more to them than all human bonds of union in creed or church order. May all who have put on the Lord Jesus above all things put on love, the bond of perfectness.

Lord Jesus! we do beseech Thee, draw Thy people in united prayer to the footstool of Thy Throne of Glory, whence Thou givest Thy Spirit to reveal Thy presence to each as present in all. Oh, fill us with Thy Spirit, and we shall be one I one Spirit and one Body. Amen.

Chapter 31
Filled With the Spirit.

'Be filled with the Spirit, speaking to one another.' Ephesians 5:18

These words are a command. They enjoin upon us, not what the state of apostles or ministers ought to be, but what should be the ordinary consistent experience of every true-hearted believer. It is the privilege every child of God may claim from his Father, to be filled with the Spirit. Nothing less will enable him to live the life he has been redeemed for, abiding in Christ, keeping His commandments, and bearing much fruit. And yet, how little this command has been counted among those which all ought to keep! How little it has been thought possible or reasonable that all should be expected to keep it !

One reason of this is undoubtedly that the words have been wrongly understood. Because with the day of Pentecost, and on more than one subsequent occasion, the being filled with the Spirit was accompanied with the manifest enthusiasm of a supernatural joy and power, such a state has been looked on as one of excitement and strain, quite inconsistent with the quiet course of ordinary life. The suddenness and the strength and the outward manifestation of the Divine impulse were so linked with the idea of being filled with the Spirit, that it was thought to be something for special occasions, a blessing only possible to a very few. Christians felt as if they could not venture, as if they did not need, to fix their hopes so high ; as if, were the blessing given to them, it would be impossible in their circumstances to maintain or to manifest it.

The message I have to bring today is that the command is indeed for every believer, and that, as wide as the precept, is the promise and the power too. May God give us grace, that our meditation on this His Word may waken in the heart of every reader, not only strong desire but the firm assurance that the privilege is meant for him, that the way is not too hard, that the blessing will in very deed yet become his own.

In a country like South Africa, where we often suffer from drought, we find two sorts of dams or reservoirs made for catching up and storing water. On some farms you have a fountain, but with a stream too weak to irrigate with. There a reservoir is made for collecting the water, and the filling of the reservoir is the result of the gentle, quiet inflow from the fountain day and night. In other cases, again,, the farm has no fountain at all ; the reservoir is built in the bed of a stream or in a hollow where, when rain falls, the water can be collected. In such a place, the filling of the reservoir, with a heavy fall of rain, is often the work of a very few hours, and is accompanied with a rush and violence not free from danger. The noiseless supply of the former farm is, at the same time, the surer, because the supply, though apparently feeble, is permanent; in tracts where the rainfall is uncertain, a reservoir may stand empty for months or years.

There is the same difference in the way in which the fullness of the Spirit comes. On the day of Pentecost, at times when new beginnings are made, in the outpouring of the Spirit of conversion in heathen lands, or of revival among Christian people, suddenly, mightily, manifestly, men are filled with the Holy Ghost. In the enthusiasm and the joy of the newly found salvation, the power of the Spirit is undeniably present. And yet, for those who receive it thus, there are special dangers. The blessing is often too much dependent on the fellowship with others, or extends only to the upper and more easily reached currents of the soul's life: the sudden is often the superficial; the depths of the will and the inner life have not been reached. Other Christians there are who have never been partakers of any such marked experience, and in whom, nevertheless, the fullness of the Spirit is no less distinctly seen in the deep and intense devotion to Jesus, in a walk in the light of His countenance and the consciousness of His Holy presence, in the blamelessness of a life of simple trust and obedience, and in the humility of a self-sacrificing love to all around. They have their types in what Barnabas was: 'a son of consolation, a good man, and full of the Holy Ghost.'

And which of these is now the true way of being filled with the Spirit? The answer is easy. There are farms on which both the above-named reservoirs are to be found, auxiliary to each other. There are even reservoirs, where the situation is favorable, in which both the modes of filling are made use of. The regular, quiet, daily in-flowing keeps them supplied in time of great drought; in time of rain they are ready to receive and store up large supplies. There are Christians who are not content but with special mighty visitations: the rushing mighty wind, floods out-poured, and the baptism of fire-these are their symbols. There are others to whom the fountain springing up from within, and quietly streaming forth, appears the true type of the Spirit's work. Happy they who can recognize God in both, and hold themselves always ready to be blessed in whichever way He comes.

And what are now the conditions of this fullness of the Spirit? God's word has one answer-faith. It is faith alone that sees and receives the Invisible, that sees and receives God Himself. The cleansing from sin and the loving surrender to obedience, which were the conditions of the first reception of the Spirit, are the fruit of the faith that saw what sin was, and what the blood, and what the will and the love of God. Of these we do not speak here again. Our text is for believers who have been faithful in their seeking to obey, and yet have not what they long for. By faith they must specially see what there is that needs to be cast out. All filling needs emptying. I do not here speak of the cleansing out of sin, and the surrender to full obedience. This is always the first essential. But I speak of believers who in this think they have done what God demands, and yet fail of the blessing. The first condition of all filling is emptiness. What is a reservoir but a great hollow, a great emptiness prepared, waiting, thirsting, crying for the water to come ? Any true abiding fullness Of the Spirit is preceded by emptying. ' I sought the blessing long and earnestly,' said one, 'and I wondered why it did not come. At last I found it was because there was no room in my heart to receive it.' In such emptying out there are various elements. A deep dissatisfaction with the religion we have hitherto had. A deep consciousness of how much there has been of the wisdom and the work of the flesh in it. A discovery, and confession, and giving up of all in life that had been kept in our own hands and management, in which self had hitherto reigned, of all in which we had not thought it necessary or possible that Jesus should directly be consulted and pleased. A deep conviction of impotence and utter helplessness to grasp or seize what is offered. A surrender, in poverty of spirit to wait on the Lord in His great mercy and power, 'according to the riches of His glory, to strengthen us mightily by His Spirit in the inner man.' A great longing, thirsting, waiting, crying, a praying without ceasing for the Father to fulfill His promise in us, and take full possession of us within. Such an emptying is on the way to the filling.

With this is needed the believing which accepts, which receives, which holds the gift. It is through faith in Christ and in the Father that the Divine fullness will flow into us. Of the same Ephesians, to whom the command is given, 'Be filled with the Spirit,' Paul had said, 'In Christ, having believed, ye were sealed with the Holy Spirit of promise.' The command refers to what they had already received: the fountain was within them ; it had to be opened up, and way made for it; it would spring up and fill their being. And yet not as if this was in their own power: Jesus had said, ' He that believeth, keeps believing in me, rivers of living water shall flow out of him.' The fullness of the Spirit is so truly in Jesus, the receiving out of Him must so really be in the unbroken continuity of a real life-fellowship, the ceaseless inflow of the sap from Him the living Vine must so distinctly be met by the ceaseless recipiency of a simple faith, that the upspringing of the fountain within can only be in the dependence on Jesus above. It is by the faith of Jesus, whose baptism with the Spirit has as distinct a commencement as His cleansing with the blood, but is also maintained by, as continuous a renewal, that the inflow will grow ever stronger until it comes to the overflowing.

And yet the faith in Jesus, and the hourly and ever-growing up-springing of the Spirit, will not dispense with faith in the Father's special gift and the prayer for His special renewed fulfillment of His promise. For these same Ephesians, who had thus the Spirit within them as the earnest of their inheritance, Paul prays to the Father ' that He would grant you, according to the riches of His glory, that ye may be strengthened with power through His Spirit in the inner man.' The verbs both denote not a gradual work, but an act, something done at once. The expression, 'according to the riches of His glory,' indicates something which is to be a great exhibition of the Divine love and power, something very special and Divine. They had the Spirit indwelling. He prayed for them that the direct interposition of the Father might give them such mighty workings of the Spirit, such a fullness of the Spirit, that the indwelling of Christ, and a life in the love that passeth knowledge, and a being filled with the fullness of God, might be their blessed personal experience. When the flood came of old, the windows of heaven above, and the fountains of the great deep beneath, were together opened. It is still so in the fulfillment of the promise of the Spirit: 'I will pour floods upon the dry ground.' The deeper and clearer the faith in the Indwelling Spirit, and the simpler the waiting on Him, the more abundant will be the renewed down-coming of the Spirit from the heart of the Father direct into the heart of His waiting child.

There is one more aspect in which it is essential to remember that this fullness comes to faith. God loves when He appears to come in lowly and unlikely appearance, to clothe Himself in the garment of humility which He wants His children to love and wear. ' The Kingdom of Heaven is like a seed:' only faith can know what glory there is in its littleness. Thus was the dwelling of the Son on earth; thus is the indwelling of the Spirit in the heart. He asks to be believed in, when nothing is seen or felt. Believe that the fountain that springs up and flows forth in living streams is within, even when all appears dry. Take time to retire into the inner chamber of the heart, and thence send up praise and offer worship to God in the assurance of the Holy Ghost within. Take time to be still and realize, and let the Spirit Himself fill thy spirit with this most spiritual and heavenly of all truths-that He dwells within thee. Not in the thoughts or feelings first, but in the life, deeper than where we can see and feel, is His temple, His hidden dwelling place. When once faith knows that it hath what it has asked, it can afford to be patient, and can abound in thanksgiving even where the flesh would murmur. It can trust the Unseen Jesus and the Hidden Spirit. It can believe in that little and unlikely seed, the smallest of all the seeds. It can trust and give glory to Him who is able to do exceeding abundantly above all it can think, and can mightily strengthen in the inner man, just when all appears feeble and ready to faint. Believer! expect not the fullness of the Spirit in the way which thy human reasoning deviseth, but even as was the coming of the Son of God without form or comeliness, in a way that is folly to human wisdom. Expect the Divine Strength in great weakness; become a fool to receive the Divine wisdom which the Spirit teacheth; be willing to be nothing, because God chooseth the things that are not to bring to nought the things that are. So shalt thou learn not to glory in the flesh, but to glory in the Lord. And in the deep joy of a life of daily obedience and childlike simplicity, thou shalt know what it is to be filled with the Spirit.

O my God ! Thy fullness of love and of glory is like a boundless ocean-infinite and inconceivable. I bless Thee that, in revealing Thy Son, it pleased Thee that all the fullness of the Godhead should dwell in Him bodily, that in Him we might see that fullness in human life and weakness. I bless Thee that His Church on earth is even now, in all its weakness, His body, the fullness of Him that filleth all in all; that in Him we are made full; that by the mighty working of Thy Spirit, and the indwelling of Thy Son, and the knowledge of Thy love, we may be filled to all the fullness of God.

Blessed Father! I thank Thee that the Holy Spirit is to us the bearer of the fullness of Jesus, and that in being filled with the Spirit we are made full with that fullness. I thank thee that there, have been men on earth since Pentecost, not a few, of whom Thou hast seen that they were full of the Holy Ghost. 0 my God ! make me full. Let the Holy Spirit take and keep possession of my deepest, inmost life. Let Thy Spirit fill my spirit.

Let thence the fountain flow through all the soul's affections and powers. Let it flow over and flow out through my lips, speaking Thy praise and love. Let the very body, by the quickening and sanctifying energy of the Spirit, be Thy temple, full of the Life Divine. Lord my God! I believe Thou hearest me. Thou hast given it me-; I accept it as mine.

Oh, grant that throughout Thy Church the fullness of the Spirit may be sought and found, may be known and proved. Lord Jesus our glorified King, oh, let Thy Church be full of the Holy Ghost. Amen.